PAUSE PATTERNS IN ELIZABETHAN AND JACOBEAN DRAMA

An Experiment in Prosody

By Ants Oras

University of Florida Monographs

HUMANITIES

No. 3, Winter 1960

UNIVERSITY OF FLORIDA PRESS/GAINESVILLE, FLORIDA

CONTENTS

Introduction   1

1. From Chaucer to Spenser   7

2. Spenser, Marlowe, and
   the 1590's   10

3. Shakespeare, Ben Jonson,
   and Donne   13

4. Other Seventeenth-Century
   Playwrights   20

5. Some Special Applications of
   the Study of Pause Patterns   30

Graphs   33

Tables   61

A Note on the Sources   89

INTRODUCTION

Renaissance prosody is a well-tilled field, but there are still some uncultivated spots in it, and also opportunities for modifying the methods of cultivation. While much labor has been expended on some of its most conspicuous areas, above all on the verse of Shakespeare, few attempts have been made to cover the entire territory from any specific angle. Besides, less attention has been paid by Renaissance scholars to the verse as verse than to prosodical analysis as a means of solving problems of chronology or authorship.

The present study proposes to examine verse as such, for its own sake, as one of the principal elements contributing to the total impact of Renaissance drama and determining the special nature of the impression that drama creates. It endeavors to make a contribution to the understanding of what Renaissance verse is and of the factors that made it develop the way it did. And the study hopes to achieve this end by concentrating on a seemingly narrow, yet essential, set of prosodical phenomena, examining them in an unusually large number of texts—virtually the entire Renaissance drama of England, omitting only minor figures. By thus in one way narrowing and in another way extending the field of vision in a manner not generally attempted, the study expects to bring out contexts not seen, or perceived but vaguely, in studies confined to more limited sections of the dramatic output of the period, or in studies relying, as so far has been the rule (apart from inquiries into Shakespearean prosody), on a sampling method incapable of accurately charting the course of development. Complete works have been examined for the material here presented; only for some of the background material have samples been used, and these were large samples.

The feature of verse chosen for examination is a rhythmical one, more instinctive and thus more expressive of basic rhythmical impulses than most—the phenomenon of pauses. "Probably the variations that most easily become unconscious are those of pausation," says Sir E. K. Chambers, and it should be difficult not to agree with him. But I intend to deal with my subject in a manner which, to my knowledge, is new in several respects. What I want to discover is configurations, fully articulated total designs. The question

1

I ask—too seldom asked by students of prosody—is not how often on the whole pauses occur in a work, but in what positions they appear in the verse, and in what ratios compared with other positions in the line. So, no attempt has been made to compute the number of pauses in relation to the total number of lines in a work, which has been the usual procedure. What has been studied is the incidence of internal pauses in each of the nine positions possible within an iambic pentameter line in relation to the totals of such pauses, regardless of the amounts represented by such totals.* Plays with only a hundred internal pauses indicated by punctuation may thus present percentage patterns identical with those of plays—or poems —having thousands of such pauses. Authors may deliberately choose to use little or much pausation in their verse, but they will generally be less aware of the positions in the line in which they pause. It is these less conscious pause patterns that I have attempted to find and analyze. Although it will become apparent that even in pause patterning there can be much deliberation, and even rigid regulation, especially as regards the main pause in a verse, the "caesura," the total patterns are likely to reveal much over which the person concerned has little or no control, almost as people are unable to control their cardiograms.

The method here used inevitably had to be statistical. Only by meticulous counting and computation could the basic patterns be detected. However, since mere figures appeal very little to the imagination of humanists, including that of the present author, the series of pedantically mathematical ratios were converted into graphs which, it is hoped, will mostly speak for themselves. Even so, some initial comments are obviously required.

Few readers will pause in exactly the same places when reading the identical passages of verse. This means that few editors, no matter how learned, read the same passage in exactly the same way. The punctuation of modern editions of Shakespeare illustrates this strikingly: Dover Wilson's *Tempest* is not quite that of Hardin Craig or that of Kittredge. Each of these scholars injects into the play something of his own rhythm—a twentieth-century rhythm. This

---

*I have used this method before in connection with Milton ("Milton's Blank Verse and the Chronology of his Major Poems" in *SAMLA Studies in Milton* [Gainesville: University of Florida Press, 1953], pp. 128-197), but without my present type of graph and not quite realizing the degree of distinctiveness which pause patterns can achieve in a writer.

has made me prefer the punctuation of the original editions, even though I am fully aware that it is not unaffected by the intervention of scribes and printers. Nevertheless, the distortions, such as they are, are distortions of the period with which I am concerned. They keep within the rhythmical climate of the time.

Pauses vary in emphasis and length. For the purposes of the present inquiry three levels of pausal emphasis are distinguished, and each of my statistical tables and graphs records a pattern of one of three kinds: (1) a pattern formed by all pauses indicated by internal punctuation (*A-patterns*); (2) a pattern of "strong pauses," i.e. pauses shown by punctuation marks other than commas (*B-patterns*); and (3) a pattern of "splits" or "line splits," i.e. breaks within the pentameter line dividing speeches by different characters —by far the heaviest type of pause, rarely found before 1600 (*C-patterns*). Where a total for any category was less than twenty, I generally refrained from making either a table or a graph. Where all percentages, however small the totals, were represented in full, as in the case of Shakespeare, certain characteristic differences emerged: the more emphatic pauses displayed sharper contrasts from work to work and from period to period. Being more deliberate, they in greater measure brought out intention, whereas the more inclusive categories more fully reflected less conscious and more stable trends—the deep underlying rhythms.

My treatment of the different periods is not uniform. For the period until about 1600 I consider all pauses shown by punctuation, and also splits where there are enough of them. In this period even strong internal punctuation can be very scarce. Greene's *Friar Bacon and Friar Bungay*, for instance, has within the line only six punctuation marks that are not commas. For cases like this I record only the A-patterns.

For the seventeenth century, on the other hand, when line splits become frequent, I examine only these splits, except in a few special cases, notably that of Shakespeare. In no instance, except for the B-sequences of Jonson, have any A- or B-data been recorded for plays whose date falls after 1616, the year of Shakespeare's death and of the publication of Ben Jonson's Folio. In addition to the impossibility of singlehandedly examining the entire punctuation of hundreds of plays, there was the difficulty of finding satisfactory editions, which are not plentiful for this period. Photostats and microfilms could not be procured in sufficient numbers.

3

Dramatic verse has too often been examined in isolation, with little reference to the possible influence exercised upon it by the verse of other genres. This is an unrealistic approach. Spenser, who never produced a play, will be found to be one of the principal figures in the present essay, a poet whose pause patterning decisively influenced the dramatic verse of the 1590's. Similarly, some important developments in blank verse would probably have been different but for the strongly anti-Spenserian influence of John Donne's early verse. For my background study I have indeed had to go as far back as Chaucer and his foreign models, and sixteenth-century French and Italian verse had to be considered. Mediaevalists and Romance scholars will doubtless be able to correct some of my findings in these more remote areas, but I hope my principal conclusions will hold good.

I have confined myself to studying lines with five *metrical* stresses (as distinguished from speech stresses)—the type commonly called iambic pentameter; but I include lines lacking the unstressed beginning, i.e. "truncated" lines, and also lines lacking one or two internal unstressed syllables, as long as the five metrical stresses remain intact. Extrametrical unstressed syllables are not counted. In the case of "epic caesuras," i.e. trochaic pauses followed by a full iambic foot, the first unstressed syllable is disregarded in the statistics. My patterns include only "internal" pauses, i.e. pauses occurring before the fifth metrical stress. Despite my attempt to be utterly consistent, there doubtless still remains some margin of error—a margin too slight, however, as I hope, to affect conclusions of any importance or appreciably to change my percentages and consequently the appearance of the graphed patterns.

In addition to the figures for each of the nine pausal positions, the tabular matter at the end of this study contains: (1) the totals for internal pauses in each work or group of works (under "Total"); (2) a percentage figure indicating the ratio of such pauses before the fifth position, i.e. in the first half of the line, to pauses after that position (under "First Half"); and (3) a figure showing the percentage of pauses in even positions, that is, pauses after an even-numbered syllable (under "Even"). The gradual shift of pauses from the earlier to the later part of the line and the decreasing importance of pauses in the normally stressed even positions during the period under examination are among the most significant phenomena to be studied in the following pages.

4

Since it is advisable that the reader should from the very start keep referring to the graphs, I explain their arrangement and nature here. Like the tables, they are arranged separately for each of the three levels (A, B, and C), in chronological order as far as was possible and seemed reasonable. Every effort has been made to represent the development of the individual authors according to the best chronologies available, but dissension among specialists sometimes has compelled me to exercise a cautious eclecticism. The graphs for the foreign poets, for Chaucer, for Spenser, and for Shakespeare have not been split up among the A-, B-, and C-series like the rest, but are kept together in each case to facilitate visual comparison at these points of crucial importance.

The graphs, one for each work, or sometimes each group of works, altogether over seven hundred, simply present the statistical data in a visual form. They are all drawn to the same scale. Height represents the percentage figures, whereas horizontal interval indicates the position in the five-stress, ten-syllable verse line—the first position, the second, the third, and so on through the ninth. I give

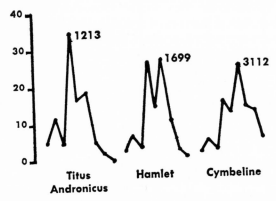

here three examples from the A-sequence for Shakespeare, for *Titus Andronicus, Hamlet,* and *Cymbeline*. The nine percentages are for *Titus Andronicus:* 4.9, 11.6, 5.4, 35.4, 17.1, 19.3, 4.7, 1.5, 0.1; for *Hamlet:* 2.5, 7.1, 3.8, 27.1, 14.9, 27.7, 11.4, 4.2, 1.1; and for *Cymbeline:* 2.0, 5.1, 3.3, 15.8, 12.5, 25.6, 15.2, 14.3, 6.2. Disregarding any decimals of fewer than five points and counting any five decimal points as a full unit, we obtain the three graphs shown here. The graph for *Titus Andronicus,* accordingly, indicates that approximately 5 per cent of all punctuation marks

5

within the five-stress lines of the play occur after the first syllable, 12 per cent occur after the second syllable, 5 per cent after the third syllable, and none after the ninth syllable; this graph has nothing to say about punctuation at the end of the line. The figures to the right, close to the top of each graph, indicate the total number of internal pauses in each work.

The reader is invited to consult the graphs constantly in the following discussion. He will find footnotes referring him to the appropriate pages where the relevant graphs are located. The discussion is indeed primarily a guide manual to the striking facts recorded in the graphs.

1. FROM CHAUCER TO SPENSER

The fact that Geoffrey Chaucer, the first distinguished writer of iambic pentameters in English, the poet who really established this form in the language, began by translating and imitating French poetry and then passed through a phase of Italian influence seems to be reflected in his pause patterns.[1] A comparison of our Chaucer graphs with the graphs for foreign poets he knew, Eustache Deschamps, Guillaume de Machaut, Petrarch, and Boccaccio,[2] shows a fairly steady change in Chaucer from French-type patterns with tall fourth-position peaks—even though not nearly as tremendous as in the French graphs—towards more varied patterns closer to those of the Italians, with lower peaks, an additional elevation in the sixth position, and higher levels for several of the other pauses. This change is less evident in the patterns of the strong pauses, where the emphasis almost throughout lies heavily on the even positions, sharply reinforcing the iambic meter, than it is in the more inclusive A-patterns. In the A-patterns the unstressed fifth-syllable pauses, and in the graphs of the later poems also those after the seventh syllable, grow more prominent; the staccato rhythm is softened, the movement of the line towards its final point becomes more fluid and unimpeded. However, from the very beginning Chaucer avoids falling into the French extreme of an absolutely obligatory fourth-position caesura. In French with its fixed word accent, this device was felt to be indispensable if a satisfactory degree of rhythmical organization was to be achieved, whereas the far more predominantly iambic rhythm peculiar to English hardly needed any caesural support of such rigidity. Italian verse, syllabic rather than syllabo-accentual in theory, in its actual rhythms often came very close to English iambics: hence, it would seem, its greater freedom in pause arrangement, which may well have influenced Chaucer. Here, too, however, Chaucer is certainly far from being a mere docile imitator: his ratios for even pauses are lower in his later patterns than those of the Italian poets; in other words, he applies less iambic emphasis, as was natural in a language itself more iambic.

It has been questioned how far the subtleties of Chaucer's metrical

1. See p. 34.   2. See p. 33.

procedures were grasped even by some of his contemporaries, not to mention his successors. The loss of the final *e* must have obscured his rhythms to many of the latter. His pauses in uneven positions can no longer have been invariably recognizable as feminine. This evidence of faulty reading does not appear from my Hoccleve sample, which comes close to the later Chaucer, but my samples from Henryson, and even from Lydgate, seem to suggest that these poets had learned little or nothing from Chaucer's handling of pauses. Here, as also in the early sixteenth-century "Bowge of Court" of Skelton, the fourth position starkly predominates, dwarfing everything else.[3]

No perceptible changes in pausal distribution are introduced by either Wyatt or Surrey.[4] The new overmastering craving for iambic regularity, after a long period of awkward mismetering, affects this aspect of versecraft, especially in their successors. The mandatory fourth-syllable caesura in iambic pentameters dominates both theory and practice. Gascoigne's *Notes of Instruction* (1575) and George Puttenham's *Arte of English Poesie* (published in 1589, but written much earlier) both clearly state the obligatory nature of this pause, although Gascoigne permits some license in "Rithme royall." Puttenham gives some reasons for his rule: (1) some breathing space is needed between syntactic subdivisions, lest these "huddle one vpon another so rudly & so fast that th' eare may not perceiue their difference"; (2) "in euery long verse the *Cesure* ought to be kept precisely, if it were but to serue as a law to correct the licentiousness of rymers, besides that it pleaseth the eare better, & sheweth more cunning in the maker by following the rule of his restraint."[5] What this amounts to is the need for some clearer demarcation of syntactic structure, and for discipline and self-control in a period still far from metrical virtuosity; a need for regularity as a restraining and controlling influence on versifiers still struggling hard to shape a seemingly unmalleable language. That the inculcation of this rule was not unconnected with French influence appears from Sidney's reference in his *Apology for Poetry* to "the *Cesura*, or breathing place, in the middest of the verse," which as he, perhaps with a touch of disparagement, remarks, "neither Italians nor Spanish haue," but which—do we hear any undertone of complacency in this addition?—"the French, and we, neuer almost fayle of."[6]

3. See pp. 35, 43. 4. See pp. 35, 43.
5. See G. G. Smith, *Elizabethan Critical Essays* (1937), I, 78-80.
6. *Ibid.*, p. 205.

The evidence proves the correctness of Sidney's statement: most of the patterns for that period look as French as those of Lydgate and Henryson or of Du Bellay and Ronsard.[7] In Gascoigne's *Steel Glass* the fourth-position top reaches a height of more than 80 per cent.[8] A study of his text shows commas to have been inserted in the caesural position even where this would seem contrary to the sense. An even more extreme example of this practice—not included in our graphs—is Thomas Churchyard's "Cardinal Wolsey," published in the 1587 edition of *The Mirror for Magistrates,* though probably composed somewhat earlier. Every single line in this pedantic poem has at least a comma after the fourth syllable, quite regardless of sense and syntax, e.g. in such lines as "But such as to, the height of ladder climes" (1. 458), or "But when the bruite, of this was blowne aboute" (1. 474). The insistence on the formal principle at the expense of the meaning is clearly deliberate here, as it is often also in dramatic blank verse, the punctuation of some of which has confused editors, making them change it along more logical but less characteristically sixteenth-century rhythmical lines. What such instances seem to suggest is a measured, declamatory, perhaps slightly chanting manner of reading, removed as far as possible from easy conversational delivery.

Some independent experimentation with pauses appears in an unexpected quarter. Nicholas Grimald, while quite as metronomically iambic as anyone else, spaces his pauses differently, over all the even positions, so that his patterns, especially the A-pattern for his rhymed verse, look as though drawn with a straightedge, descending in almost exactly mathematical proportion from the fourth to the sixth to the eighth position, with deep incisions in between for the uneven pauses.[9] Since Grimald's punctuation is unusually heavy, the numerous masculine pauses—sometimes three or four in a line —almost unbearably accentuate the iambic monotony. Decades later very similar patterns appear in two writers whom one would not otherwise tend to link: in Thomas Hughes' uninspired, if not unscholarly, *Misfortunes of Arthur,* and—perhaps not surprisingly in view of his pronouncement on caesuras—in Sir Philip Sidney's *Astrophel and Stella.*

7. See pp. 33, 35, 43.   8. See pp. 35, 43.
9. See pp. 35, 43.

9

2. SPENSER, MARLOWE,
AND THE 1590's

The turning point came where one would expect it: in the verse of the New Poet.[1] The essential innovations of Spenser in regard to pause patterning are two: (1) instead of one peak, after the fourth syllable, he usually has two, for a second though lower one generally appears after the sixth syllable; (2) his fifth-position depression is markedly raised in the A-patterns, so that in four cantos of *The Faerie Queene*—in the Bower of Bliss canto (II.xii); the Thames and Medway wedding canto (IV.xi); the canto recounting Artegall's fight with Grantorto (V.xii); and the canto lyrically describing the home of the Graces and their dancing (VI.x)— it entirely disappears, making the graph slope gently down from the fourth position to the ninth, with no intervening hollows or notches. The poetic effect corresponds to the visual impression; the jagged, spiky ultra-iambic stiffness is gone. Two at least of the mentioned four cantos—II.xii and IV.xi—are showpieces of luxuriant description and soft music, of that "golden style" which C. S. Lewis contrasts with the "drab style" of earlier poets. It may be of some significance that this manner, which is rather less apparent in Spenser's earlier work, happened to reach its full development at a time when he was deep in the Italians, especially Ariosto. As in the case of Chaucer two centuries earlier, Italian studies seem to have led English verse towards freer and more varied artistry.

As an illustration of the distance Spenser has traveled from the drumming beat of the school of stern iambic consistency, I compare a stanza from the catalogue of the Nereides in the Thames and Medway wedding procession with a passage from Grimald.

> White hand *Eunica*, proud *Dynamene*,
> Ioyous *Thalia*, goodly *Amphitrite*,
> Louely *Pasithee*, kinde *Eulimene*,
> Light foote *Cymothoe*, and sweete *Melite*,
> Fairest *Pherusa*, *Phao* lilly white,
> Wondred *Agaue*, *Poris*, and *Nesæa*,
> With *Erato* that doth in loue delite,
> And *Panopæ*, and wise *Protomedæa*,
> And snowy neckd *Doris*, and milkewhite *Galathæa*.
>   (*F.Q.*IV.xi.49)

1. See pp. 35-40.

Now corpses hide the purpurde soyle with blood:
Large slaughter on ech side: but Perses more
Moyst feelds bebledd: their herts, and noombers bate.
Fainted while they giue back, and fall to fight:
The lightning Macedon, by swoords, by gleaus,
By bands, and trowps, of fotemen with his garde,
Speeds to Darie: but him, his nearest kyn,
Oxate preserues, with horsemen on a plump
Before his carr: that none the charge could giue.

(Death of Zoroas, 19-27)

Grimald's vigorous if undistinguished verse moves with mono-syllabic choppiness, cut up into small iambic phrasal groups and quite devoid of any feminine softness or feminine pauses. Spenser's richly polysyllabic passage seems to flow, even to soar and sing; over half the pauses are feminine, coming after the fifth, and in one instance the seventh, syllable; no abrupt breaks keep the lines from moving easily to their end.

This lyrical mellowness—not Spenser's staple style, which has a more iambic movement—seems to be the quality of his verse that most deeply affected his contemporaries, apparently even before his great poem was accessible in print. Marlowe's well-known echoes from Spenser in the first *Tamburlaine* prove the early circulation of at least some of the work. After 1590 Spenser's subtler method almost completely ousts the obtrusive iambic bleakness of the "drab style."

Kyd's *Spanish Tragedy* and Marlowe's *Tamburlaine*[2] show the impact of the Bower of Bliss pattern. In *The Jew of Malta* and *Dr. Faustus* Marlowe even goes far beyond Spenser in the use of feminine pauses—needless to say, not in order to achieve softness but lyrical *élan* and greater momentum. In *Edward II* where the momentum is perceptibly reduced, and in the formal rhymed poetry of Marlowe, the average Spenserian pattern reappears. It may well have been in part indirectly, through the medium of Marlowe's heady blank verse and to a less degree through Kyd's verse, that Spenser's manner of pause patterning suddenly spread into the drama.

A glance at the A-patterns of Robert Greene provides a good example of what happened. In *Alphonsus of Aragon*, and in *A Looking Glass for London* which Greene wrote with Lodge, the

2. See pp. 41, 43, 44.

fourth-position peaks rise up very steeply, but then they conspicuously subside. The pattern of *Friar Bacon and Friar Bungay* might belong to Marlowe. So might that of Lodge's unaided *Wounds of Civil War*. George Peele, too, quickly falls in line.[3] His last two plays show no indentations in the gradually descending right-hand slopes of their A-graphs. Even the rugged verse of *Arden of Feversham* uses pauses in Spenser's usual manner or in that of *Edward II*. The exceptions to the new tendency seem few and far between.

An instructive case is that of *Gismond of Salerne* (1566) and its later revision in awkward blank verse, Robert Wilmot's *Tancred and Gismund* (1591). Wilmot, somewhat reducing the iambic jaggedness of the pattern, comes closer to Spenser.[4] Nevertheless, even his A-pattern remains very sharply indented. This may be partly because he had not completely discarded rhyme. Although our graphs for rhymed and unrhymed verse in this period look remarkably alike, a study of the percentages for even pauses will show that these, on the whole, are higher in rhymed pentameters. Rhyme apparently slightly impeded freedom of experimentation, whereas blank verse as the less traditional form encouraged it.

Similar considerations seem to apply to Fulke Greville's two plays, discussed here because at least *Mustapha* apparently was originally composed before the turn of the century.[5] Greville's style, conservative also in other respects, retains a large proportion of rhyme, even though in new, experimental arrangements. The pause patterns of this aristocratically aloof writer seem to be harking back to those of Hughes, Grimald, and Sidney, from which they hardly differ except for their lower fourth-position peaks.

Despite such isolated survivals of an old style, the Spenserian fashion triumphs in a manner soon resulting in a new monotony. The same patterns, now turned into period patterns, especially that of the Bower of Bliss canto and *Tamburlaine*, appear almost everywhere. The only great metrical revolutionary of the younger generation, John Donne, whose pause arrangements are very different, as yet hardly affects the drama.

3. See pp. 41, 44.   4. See pp. 41, 43.
5. See pp. 42, 45.

3. SHAKESPEARE, BEN JONSON, AND DONNE

W e are now approaching the center of the picture, the work of Shakespeare. Even a casual glance at the Shakespeare graphs shows him at first to have been anything but an innovator: for the most part he clearly follows Spenser's, or possibly Marlowe's, lead. Since the exact order of composition of some of his work is still uncertain, only an approximate account of his evolution in any area can be attempted. Even so, it can be claimed that there is more over-all steadiness of development and firmness of direction in the long succession of his pause patterns than in those of any other writer examined in this monograph. Covering more than two decades, his patterns in an individual way epitomize, and often anticipate, the development of a large part of the blank verse written in that time of great and rapid creative advance. They present a picture of organic growth, a process ending only with the end of his career, even though the changes become much less pronounced in his latest plays. (See pages 46-52.)

Of the three series of patterns, which are all given here in full even where the totals are low, the most inclusive one, the A-pattern, shows the greatest continuity. The ups and downs in contiguous patterns are slight, their earlier sixteenth-century shapes nearly all remaining Marlovian or Spenserian, but interestingly enough with only some occasional appearances of the most prevalent type of the period. The peaks gradually subside in the fourth position, rising in the sixth, until at the turn of the century a complete balance is reached. A rise in the unstressed fifth position takes it a few times —in *1 Henry VI*, *A Midsummer-Night's Dream,* and *King John*— above the sixth, producing the pattern most in vogue at the time. After *Hamlet* the course of development becomes somewhat less straight. This period of profound struggle, violent contrasts, sublime tragedies, and bitter comedies shows deepening, sharpening fifth-position clefts and some back-and-forth in the position of the highest points, but with a continuing general trend towards predominance of the sixth position, which emphatically culminates at the time of the great cathartic plays *King Lear* and *Macbeth*. From then on, the peaks—now invariably in the sixth position—slowly decline, while the unstressed seventh position close to the end of the line gains some height.

Almost the same description could be given of Shakespeare's B-patterns, save that the contrasts are a little sharper, the iambic peaks taller, the trochaic troughs deeper, the continuity is less steady, and a preliminary fourth-and-sixth-position balance is reached already in the *Merchant of Venice*. The strong pauses, moreover, are more definitely concentrated into the middle of the line, suggesting a tendency to avoid sharper breaks very early or very late in the verse.

Greater idiosyncrasies appear in the C-patterns, those for line splits, where the explanation for their irregularity especially in the earlier graphs of the sequence may partly lie in the low totals there —only seventeen splits in the *Comedy of Errors*, only thirteen in the *Merry Wives*. A few units may cause considerable changes in the percentages here. This circumstance somewhat obscures the picture of development, which, however, becomes much clearer as the series progresses. It emerges with particular clarity as soon as the plays are grouped according to periods and to genres within the periods. An interesting fact appearing from these group patterns[1] is that the histories and tragedies before *Hamlet* tend to place their pauses in a more conservative fashion than the comedies, in which the poet seems to follow his impulses more freely: the patterns of these latter seem to develop a little in advance of the graver and more formal plays. The opposite is true of the comedy usually considered to come immediately after *Hamlet*, *Troilus and Cressida*.[2] It is in some measure a throwback to an earlier manner of pause patterning. This may be connected with the parodistic spirit, the mockery of pompous heroics apparent throughout the play, which in a variety of ways brings about a sardonic revival of the style of the poet's own earlier histories. *Measure for Measure*, and especially *All's Well*, again seem to be running ahead of the dates usually assigned to them. Here, however, we are on unsafe ground: misdating has been suspected for some time at least in regard to the latter comedy. Its pause patterns would put it close to *Macbeth*.

The two features most immediately apparent in Shakespeare's use of internal pauses are: (1) the peculiar changes in his employment of uneven pauses, that is, pauses after odd-numbered syllables, whose relative frequencies increase until about the turn of the century, but then quite noticeably drop, to rise again from *Pericles* and

1. See pp. 51, 52.   2. See pp. 46, 47, 48.

Antony and Cleopatra onwards; and (2) the astonishingly steady downward course in the curve for pauses in the first half of the line, a decrease which continues throughout his career, bringing the percentages for such pauses within the totals of all pauses in the A-series down from 57.3 in *Titus Andronicus* to only 26.2 in *Cymbeline* and 21.9 in *Henry VIII*; in the B- and C-series the contrast is even more pronounced.

The former phenomenon seems the more easily explainable of the two. Feminine pauses with the opportunities they afford for suggesting unobtrusive grace contribute to that air of effortless ease which Shakespeare seems to be deliberately seeking, and certainly soon achieves, in his earlier work. From *Hamlet* to *Macbeth* the experiences he conveys are altogether more massive and disturbing, demanding more vigorous means of expression—such as, among other things, the masculine pauses, which he now increasingly uses. After *Macbeth* the tide of emotion recedes and the sharp emphases subside.

The shift towards the second half of the pentameter line presents more complex problems. The beginnings of this trend in Spenser and other Elizabethans offer no real puzzles. The rigid rule of a fourth-position caesura had led to a degree of pausal monotony against which a reaction was inevitable. Yet by the time Shakespeare was writing *Hamlet*, no traces of such monotony survived in his verse. Nevertheless, the process continued until in *Henry VIII* a new sixth-and-seventh-position monotony seemed imminent. Why?

The urge of craftsmanship, the desire to explore possibilities of new effects, may have something to do with this tendency. The earlier Elizabethans fell curiously shy of pausing anywhere after the fourth position. When they wanted less usual pauses, they introduced them in the second, and not infrequently even in the first, position; but the latter half of the line was usually kept studiously free from any breaks that might interrupt the progress of the verse. The most daring pre-Spenserian experimentalist in pause patterning, Grimald, still in his rhymed verse introduces pauses nearly as often after the second syllable as after the sixth. The effects achievable by pausing late in the line had hardly been tried. Shakespeare tried them. They attracted him so much that eventually he seemed to be getting close to the point of giving up first-half-line pauses altogether. What was the attraction?

A strong pause after the sixth syllable still does not unbalance the pentameter line; the line keeps its self-contained symmetry. Enough space is left for a complete clause to be introduced, a substantial statement to be made, before the end of the line is reached. But when such a pause comes after the seventh, or even the eighth, syllable, the remaining space usually suffices only for a fragmentary statement which needs to be completed in the following line. In other words, very late pauses make for a run-on technique.[3] Shakespeare's run-on lines, carefully counted by several scholars and conveniently tabulated, e.g., by Sir E. K. Chambers, present a curve of increasing frequencies which happen to run so closely parallel to my own ratios for second-half-line pauses in relation to first-half-line pauses that mere coincidence seems inconceivable.[4] Run-on lines and late pauses increase in frequency simultaneously and to a closely comparable extent, while the percentages for early pauses correspondingly drop. There are discrepancies, but they are slight. The two phenomena are doubtless connected—certainly in Shakespeare. We shall find occasion for doubting such a connection in the case of at least one other writer, but in regard to Shakespeare this doubt seems impossible.

Further considerations suggest themselves. After a line has achieved a certain momentum, for which space is needed, a pause, especially a strong masculine pause, cutting into the vigorous rhythmical movement, strikes the reader or listener with greater unexpectedness and seems more emphatic. The surprise effect must have been even greater in a period that had only recently learned to use any kind of pause in the second half of the line. This may help to explain the tall sixth-position peaks in the B- and C-

3. See, e.g., *The Tempest*, I. ii. 450-56:
> They are both in eythers pow'rs: But this swift business
> I must vneasie make, least the light winning
> Make the prize light. One word more: I charge thee
> That thou attend me: Thou do'st heere vsurpe
> The name thou ow'st not, and hast put thy selfe
> Vpon this Island, as a spy, to win it
> From me, the Lord on't.

It should be added that very early pauses coming after a run-on line ending increase the effect in much the same way as very late pauses. This latter type of intensified enjambment does not seem to have been used in English to any marked extent before *Paradise Lost*, where much of the special rhythm of the poem depends on it. See my paper in *SAMLA Studies in Milton*, p. 143, and E. P. Morton, *The Technique of English Non-Dramatic Blank Verse* (1910), the chapter on caesuras.

4. See p. 60.

sequences for *King Lear* and *Macbeth*. If these later subside, whereas the relatively unemphatic seventh position rises, this seems fully in keeping with the temper of Shakespeare's latest plays.

Some attention needs to be paid also to the growing frequency of extra-metrical syllables and feminine endings as Shakespeare's career progresses. Such additional syllables make it possible to crowd more matter into a line, or any part of a line. In Shakespeare's late plays the metrical demand for three or four syllables may in fact be met by some five to six syllables, and more may be said in them than in the corresponding portion of a strictly regular line. Even the last third of a line thus expanded may accommodate as much matter as a full half-line or more. A pause theoretically close to the end of a line may thus actually be removed from it by a considerable number of syllables, all capable of communicating something.

A point of some interest appears as one compares Shakespeare's rhymed pentameters with his blank verse.[5] As in the case of Marlowe, the poems show a more conservative structure than the plays would make one expect for that period, with high ratios for the even pauses and pauses in the first half of the line. The rhymed verse in the early plays, on the other hand, generally differs relatively little from the unrhymed portions; its rhythm usually blends subtly with that of the blank verse in which it is embedded, except when Shakespeare deliberately seeks contrasts, as in the case of the artisans' play in *A Midsummer Night's Dream*, where an awkward older style of verse is successfully parodied. Here the pattern becomes jagged and obtrusively iambic, with the second position leaping up to an anachronistic height.

Shakespeare's principal rival in contemporary fame, Ben Jonson, starting later, begins at a different point and subsequently develops very differently.[6] His earliest patterns on the whole resemble those of Shakespeare for the last years of the century, showing a marked tendency to balance their fourth- and sixth-position peaks. But there are important contrasts. The uneven positions reach a higher level, but the peaks of the patterns are lower than in Shakespeare. Throughout Jonson's career, with the sole exception of the 1616 text of *Everyman in His Humour*, the B-ratios for the uneven positions taken as a whole exceed 40 per cent, and in the A-sequences, here given up to 1616, the uneven positions never fall below 43 per cent, which is Shakespeare's maximum before *Henry VIII*. Thus

5. See pp. 49-50.   6. See pp. 42, 45, 53.

Jonson shows almost as many pauses at his uneven positions as at his even. His highest peaks, on the other hand, in the B-sequences never rise above 27.3, and in the A-sequences never above 24.3. Even in his most balanced period, Shakespeare's B-minimum for the highest points in his patterns is 27.6, that is, higher than Jonson's maximum, and his A-minimum is 24.3. In his late plays the apexes in the B-patterns sometimes rise to almost 50 per cent. They tower like spires over Jonson's flat though firmly built roofs.

The explanation for this lies in the unusual evenness of Jonson's pause distribution. The levels differ remarkably little in the three central positions and are relatively very high also in the three positions of the last third of the line. The percentages for the latter, if added up, already in *A Tale of a Tub* and *The Case Is Altered* exceed all corresponding Shakespearean A- and B-percentages before *All's Well*, where the A-figure is 21.5. In *Sejanus* the A-figure for these three positions is 32.1, in *Volpone* it rises to 37.4, in *The Alchemist* to 40.9. This is what makes the descents of Jonson's graphs so gradual and keeps their final points so hanging in mid-air. There is seldom any decisive predominance at any one point.

It seems impossible to find any precedent for this combination of characteristics in the drama, but very similar features occur in the early poetry of John Donne, for whose genius Jonson repeatedly, both in verse and in prose, expressed great if not unqualified admiration.[7] In his "Satires," his "Elegies," and some of his "Letters to Several Personages" Donne also in his metrical procedures does the opposite of nearly everything characteristic of the dominant Spenserian school. This is true also of his pauses. They occur abundantly all over the line, pauses in the last third of the line become exceptionally frequent, and a far more than Spenserian predilection is shown for the uneven pauses. The iambic pompousness which still somewhat persists in many of Spenser's followers has quite disappeared. The tone becomes almost that of colloquial prose. No sustained dominant emphases orchestrate the cadences of this verse. The pausal peaks—if the slight jags forming the highest points in Donne's early A-patterns may be called peaks—are as low as those of Jonson's early period.

Especially the A-graph for Donne's "Satires"—the work which Jonson sent to Lady Bedford with a poem of high praise—curiously resembles the graphs for Jonson's early work: it looks squat, spread

7. See pp. 42, 45.

18

out and strangely undecided in its outline. The picture changes in Donne's later poems—especially the "Holy Sonnets"—which revert to a type of firm design, with iambic peaks, in some instances reminiscent of Spenser, but Jonson retains his rather flat-roofed pattern. The distinctness and uniformity of its structure increase from *Sejanus* and *Volpone* onwards, suggesting perfect control and unshakable routine, but nothing even remotely resembling the all-pervasive central impulses which seem to have shaped Shakespeare's patterns for *King Lear* and *Macbeth*.

4. OTHER SEVENTEENTH-
CENTURY PLAYWRIGHTS

Jonson is the only writer I have encountered whose pause structure seems to have been noticeably influenced by Donne. John Marston, militantly antiromantic like Donne and in many ways close to Donne in his consciously roughened versification, especially in the satires of his *Scourge of Villainy* (1598), nonetheless in his pause arrangements remains conspicuously conservative to the end, carrying typical patterns of the 1590's well into the next century.[1] Only some of his earlier line-split patterns spread their pauses a little like Donne, suggesting deliberate experimentation with this extremely emphatic type, but still showing more concentration on the stressed positions of the iambic scheme. Except for these instances, he follows Spenserian and Marlovian precedents at a time when this style had been almost completely abandoned elsewhere.

Here we have reached the problem of split lines, which soon after the turn of the century began to occur abundantly in dramatic blank verse. In the earlier drama, whether academic or popular, such lines are scarce. Outside of Shakespeare I have found only a handful of sixteenth-century plays with twenty or more line splits.[2] The declamatory style then mainly affected favored resounding line-end conclusions for speeches. Where the pursuit of special effects, or perhaps more often lack of skill, caused a speech to conclude with a fragment of a line, such a line is seldom integrated into the metrical scheme. Series of short speeches are frequently arranged as ponderous stichomythia, or when they do not fill complete lines they often form special metrical patterns of their own (e.g. repeatedly in Shakespeare's early work). Senecan successions of short speeches—several to a line, and adding up to complete pentameters —at points of great dramatic tension occur in some quantity in *The Misfortunes of Arthur*[3] and *The Spanish Tragedy*, but this practice

1. See pp. 42, 45, 53.   2. See p. 52.
3. Compare, e.g., III. i. 150-55:
   Put case you winne, what griefe. / Admit I doe,
   What ioy? / Then may you rule. / When I may die. /
   To rule is much. / Small if we couet naught. /
   Who couets not a Crowne./He that discernes
   The swoord aloft. / That hangeth fast. / But by
   A haire. / Right holdes it vp. / Wrong puls it downe./

remained rare.[4] Only as the pursuit of metrical variety and the skill in handling verse gradually advanced did the dramatic impact of lines split up between speakers, yet kept within the total metrical structure, begin to be more fully exploited. The greater speed and sharpness of repartee, the rhythmical accentuation of clashes between characters made possible by this device, presently led playwrights to use it very freely and develop its technique to a remarkable degree of virtuosity. The totals of line splits in Shakespeare illustrate their growing popularity. For *Titus Andronicus* the figure is 18, for the *Merchant of Venice*, 75. But soon the figures rise into the hundreds. They are, e.g.: for *Hamlet*, 197; for *Othello*, 252; for *Antony and Cleopatra*, 461. The highest total of splits I have found anywhere is 933 for Jonson's *Alchemist*, but throughout the second and third decades of the century figures between 300 and 600 seem the rule. In the plays of John Fletcher, who liked concentrations of extreme effects, there are many pages in which only a few lines remain completely unsplit. Lines split two or three times are no longer exceptional. Playing with them often becomes a kind of game which, when excessively indulged in, leads to a new type of staccato monotony, a striving for pointed vivacity that seems forced.[5]

Being very conspicuous, line splits, as already suggested, are more deliberate than other pauses, but where there are many of them, they still tend to form characteristic patterns suggestive of more deep-seated configurations of rhythmical impulses. The material here collected suggests this clearly enough, especially where a comparison of all three levels of pauses has been possible. Although there is no complete parallelism between the three, the general tendencies nearly always are the same, provided the totals are sufficiently high to be statistically representative.

The degree of individuality in line-split patterns will be seen to vary greatly. The personal style in them generally appears only after a period of imitative apprenticeship echoing various dominant patterns of the time. Where a marked individual manner appears

4. See p. 52.
5. For this technique in Fletcher see, e.g., *The Mad Lover*, III.i:
     Ye have undone all. / So I fear. / She loves ye. /
     And then all hopes lost this way. / Peace she rises. /
     Now for my purpose Fortune. / Where's the Gentleman? /
     Gone Madam. / Why gone. / H'as dispatch't his business. /
     He came to speak with me, he did. / He did not. /

to be emerging almost at once, as in the case of Massinger, the explanation may lie in the fact that not all data are available. Massinger's beginnings, hidden away in work done in collaboration with others, are difficult or impossible to trace: what we see is already the mature, fully developed writer.

The development of a personal style seems to be impeded by collaboration in the early stages of one's career, and collaboration in general appears to have a way of toning down a writer's idiosyncrasies. The complete rhythmical unfolding of personality occurs mainly in unassisted work, especially if much of it is produced continuously over a considerable period of time. This seems to be well illustrated by the interesting case of John Fletcher. Recognizably his as his verse usually is in the early plays written with Beaumont, it develops no distinctive split-line patterning until somewhat later, when he worked mainly on his own for a number of years. In the plays he wrote with Massinger after his manner was fully established, the patterns in the graphs for his shares are nearly always unmistakably his. The contrasts with Massinger are clearly marked, yet still somewhat less clearly than in the work done independently by both.[6] Massinger's patterns here somewhat approach those of Fletcher by showing lower figures for splits in the second half of the line and in uneven positions than is usual with him. Here it seems to have been Fletcher who influenced his collaborator. On the other hand, in the much-debated matter of Fletcher's collaboration with Shakespeare in *Henry VIII*, which falls in an early phase of Fletcher's career, when his full personal manner was only beginning to show itself, he seems to have been the junior partner who had his peculiarities subdued—in this instance, however, without his pause patterns being affected: they are already characteristically his own, with the tell-tale, and quite un-Shakespearean, predominance of the seventh position which we find in him in those very years and with a markedly lower concentration into one peak than in any late work of Shakespeare's. While Fletcher does attain individuality in his patterns, Beaumont, who worked alone on only a few occasions, never reaches that point. He has only a variety of somewhat indefinitely related patterns nearly all common in his period.[7]

Our discussion of Shakespeare has already touched on some of the main points of pause patterning characteristic of the first ten

6. See pp. 55-57.   7. See p. 57.

or twelve years of the century, which also apart from Shakespeare was a time of rapid advance and experimentation in verse technique. After the close of Shakespeare's career the pace of development slows down perceptibly, perhaps partly at least because there was no one of comparable stature and unflagging resiliency of mind to take the lead. As in Shakespeare, the peaks of the graphs for the other playwrights throughout the first decades of the century move closer to the end of the line, at first to the stressed, emphatic sixth position, then with increasing frequency to the weak seventh. The uneven positions, the feminine pauses, come to be favored to a considerably greater extent than in the latest Shakespearean plays. At the same time the high points in the patterns tend to be much lower: the dominant pausal emphases are less pronounced, the contrasts in the distribution of pauses decrease.

A special kind of pattern—approximately the Bower of Bliss pattern in reverse, with a gradual ascent up to the sixth or seventh position, sometimes showing distinctive curves and bulges on the way up, then dropping off suddenly—becomes widely current. Its most obvious difference from the late Shakespearean type lies in the absence of a sharp notch or depression in the middle, in the unstressed fifth position, which generally rises above the emphatic fourth. As in the Bower of Bliss pattern, the smoothness of its shape corresponds to the smoothness of movement towards the end of the line which it represents. The differences between its highest levels are more marked, its apex is more prominent than in the flat- or round-topped Jonsonian type. Also it has far lower levels for the last positions in the line: its drops from the top usually are almost vertical. As far as I have been able to discover, its first appearance is in Dekker's *Old Fortunatus* (1599).[8] George Chapman has it in *The Gentleman Usher* (1602?) and later in *Byron* (1607).[9] Thereafter it becomes very common in Webster, Middleton, Massinger and Ford,[10] almost dominating the period. Massinger very seldom deviates from it. His patterns mostly climb up steadily to the seventh position, then fall off in a sheer drop to the eighth, and again from the eighth position almost to zero. The typical pattern of the mature Middleton is very similar, but his graphs have a special physiognomy of their own, which usually makes them immediately distinguishable from those of Massinger. They mostly culminate at the stressed sixth position, show a much steeper rise

8. See p. 53.   9. See p. 52.   10. See pp. 56-59.

from the fifth position to the top, and drop even more suddenly from the seventh to the eighth. Their upper part tends to be slimmer and more pointed, which makes them look strangely elegant. The iambic element is more prominent in Middleton's line splits than in those of most of the other writers using this type.

Fletcher, at the time that he begins to form a line-split distribution of his own, in one instance—his share in *Henry VIII*—has the general pattern just described. However, his fifth position here is only very slightly elevated above the fourth. Very soon this position declines, forming a gradually deepening notch, while the fourth and sixth positions rise: the iambic emphasis increases. By the time of his collaboration with Massinger, about and after 1620, the notch has become a deep incision: the unstressed middle position has dropped very low. Except for the less elevated sixth-position peaks, some of his patterns for this period are very like those of Shakespeare's late plays. Fletcher is on the point of overcoming the Jacobean trochaic obsession.

This obsession takes its most exaggerated form in some of the work of the most prolific playwright of the time, the man who claimed he had had "either an entire hand, or at least a maine finger" in two hundred and twenty plays, Thomas Heywood.[11] Heywood—like present-day writers of song hits—must have had a keen ear for the popular verse tunes of his time but failed to distinguish or did not care about the period's subtler rhythms. On a number of occasions he simplifies these rhythms to the point of grotesque crudity in his line splits, which soon begin to abound in his plays and are often handled with obvious deliberation and a shrewd eye for immediately striking effects. Less stable in his patterning than anybody else, not excluding Beaumont, he runs into extremes. In an early play of his, the first part of *Edward IV* (1600?), he has a fourth-position top so tall and tapering as to suggest the pre-Marlovian patterns of the 1580's.[12] In his later career he surprises us with equally towering tops, but farther to the right, in the position that had become the popular favorite, the seventh, as though deliberately caricaturing the prevailing trend. In *The Captives* (1624?) and *The English Traveller* (1633), for instance, the change from iambic to trochaic pauses, the concentration of line splits into the last third of the line are carried to absurd lengths. Since the splits in these plays are numerous—over 400 in each—

11. See pp. 54-55.   12. See p. 54.

the result is hypnotic rhythmical sameness: one nearly always knows in advance with what kind of cadence a speech is going to end; vainly hoping for some variation, one is constantly disappointed. In a much less crude way the same sort of effect is often produced in the plays of Massinger and in some of the work of Ford and the later Webster.

In connection with the constant shift towards the end of the line of Shakespeare's pauses it was pointed out that what was said about the interdependence of internal pause arrangements and the use of run-on lines did not appear to apply to all writers of the period. There is indeed at least one exception to the rule there described, namely Fletcher. One of the most immediately noticeable features among many striking peculiarities of his verse is the unusual scarcity of run-on lines. When he concludes his speeches close to line-end, as he quite often does, he plainly does not do it in order to push the reader, or pull the listener, precipitately into the next line. His line-endings tend to be heavily, often top-heavily, marked and underscored by extremely strong stresses to make readers linger over them. By accumulating closely cognate sounds, vowels as well as consonants, into the last few syllables, he seems of set purpose to create difficulties for enunciation, at least for unduly hurried enunciation that might blur the strong final effect. The brief verse segments coming after a late pause are carefully fenced off from the following line both by punctuation and by the use of double and triple endings which prevent the iambic or anapaestic lilt from being continued without interruption into the next verse. This is the very opposite of a technique intent on run-on effects. Nevertheless, for a period of several years and in some of his most characteristic work, Fletcher's favorite position for line splits is the seventh, and even afterwards it never recedes beyond the sixth. Splits later in the line are also numerous.

The explanation is probably found in the special "tune" of Fletcher's verse—an extremely powerful, almost incantatory rhythm, usually in three waves, with three very prominent stress peaks, placed on the second or fourth, the sixth or eighth, and the tenth syllables.[13] These sharply marked peaks make the typical verse of

13. Few critics of Fletcher have failed to feel this rhythm. A signal exception is Saintsbury who in his *History of English Prosody* treats Beaumont and Fletcher as more or less interchangeable prosodically (vol. II, pp. 303-4). Illuminating remarks on the subject have recently been made by Eugene M.

Fletcher predominantly dipodic, almost like the iambic trimeter of the ancients. The unusual strength of the main stresses easily carries a considerable amount of extra syllables both within the line and at its end and permits Fletcher to weight some of the metrically unstressed syllables to an extent seldom risked by other writers, yet without disturbing the clear-cut structure of the line. The varying number and arrangement of the extra syllables and the spondaic modifications add some, but not enough, diversity to this persistently recurring rhythm: pauses must be abundantly used to increase it. These pauses, if too often introduced early, would weaken the growing momentum of the rhythm, which is indispensable for the special effect characteristic of this prosody. Coming late on the vigorously rising rhythmical waves, they enliven the verse. Most of the interesting moves in Fletcher's verse seem to come late in the line, or to prepare the way for the final effect, e.g. his alliterations, which I have discussed from this point of view in an earlier study.[14]

The peculiar nature of Fletcher's verse distinguishes it sharply from everybody else's, but this nature appears with particular clarity if compared with that of his collaborator, Massinger. In some ways, especially in his use of feminine endings, Massinger comes close to Fletcher and may have been influenced by him, but in most other respects his versification stands at the opposite pole from Fletcher's. His verse has often, and rightly, been found to sound almost like prose. It has no perceptible "tune," much less the tune of an incantation. Its rhythm is not firmly marked by strong stresses, but, perhaps in order to retain enough basic regularity, keeps closer to decasyllabism. Run-on lines, often of an extreme type, with num-

---

Waith, *The Pattern of Tragicomedy in Beaumont and Fletcher* (1952), pp. 192 ff. Waith sees three main features in Fletcher's incantatory rhythm: (1) repetition, (2) repetition of stressed words in an unstressed position, producing "syncopation," and (3) alliterative emphasis on the sound and stress pattern. This pattern—he describes it simply as a "five-foot" one, without mentioning its dipodic nature—is "reinforced by frequent parallels of construction." I quote a couple of split lines typical of the structure of three "centroids" (as Craig La Drière would call them) thus reinforced:

It cannot be, it must not be. / 'Tis true, Madam.
(*Women Pleased*, III.iii)
Where is the boy? / The Boy, Sir? / I, the boy, Sir.
(*The Pilgrim*, IV.iii)

14. "Extra Monosyllables in Henry VIII and the Problem of Authorship," *JEGP*, LII (1953), 198-213. See especially pp. 205-6. See pp. 209-10 on the crowding of similar sounds at line-end.

erous "light" and "weak" endings, make his syntactically far more complex, frequently parenthetic sentences move without impediment through sequences of closely welded lines. A peculiarity of his, noted by E. H. C. Oliphant, is his disinclination to make the ends of his speeches coincide with the end of a line.[15] His speeches most frequently stop after the seventh metrical syllable, whereupon the next speech usually continues through several verses, eventually to stop again in the same position. The impression is that of a chain of uniformly shaped links that does not end. There are few real rhythmical rests. The effect is hovering, hesitantly inconclusive, and often monotonous, especially since the more robust iambic splits, as well as any splits after the seventh position, are very rare. Massinger plays safe by keeping his strong breaks clear of the two extremes of the line, but while this doubtless contributes to saving his verse from the danger of disintegration, it often leaves it rather flat and expressionless. Somewhat neutral and detached, and with a fully formed routine of his own, he produces practically the same pause pattern in play after play, almost without any development. His personality, signally lacking in Fletcherian gusto, is thus reflected in his handling of pauses as in other aspects of his verse.

The only playwright I know except the later Heywood who is even more consistent than Massinger in avoiding splits after the seventh position is Middleton in his fully formed style. Yet the impression he creates is of more emphatic pausing, of more abrupt breaks—no doubt because of his more frequent use of the even positions for his splits: their ratios normally exceed those in Massinger by some 10 to 15 per cent. By moderating the trochaic trend of the period in his own practice, he does much to keep the movement of his blank verse lively and strong.

John Webster is a poet who in two of his plays rises to impressive heights of strength and originality, but it is in these very plays, *The White Devil* and *The Duchess of Malfi*, that his patterns show no clear physiognomy of their own. His first tragedy has a variant of the inverted Bower of Bliss pattern, whereas that of its successor, with the top of its graph flattened at the fourth, fifth, sixth, and seventh positions, somewhat resembles Jonson: no emphasis dominates. This, however, may be found to agree with the depressed, mentally groping nature of the play, which one tends to forget about

15. E. H. C. Oliphant, *The Plays of Beaumont and Fletcher* (1927), pp. 59-60.

because of the power put into the great moments of a few scenes. In the plays written by Webster in collaboration with others he has more firmness and consistency of design, with seventh-position tops in the manner of Massinger—routine, one suspects, after the intense though inconclusive struggles of the early work which secured a measure of greatness for the poet. As in Massinger, the scarcity of splits after the seventh position may be due to caution on the part of a writer whose verse is not built very strongly.

The utter contrast in the patterns of the two plays usually associated with Cyril Tourneur's name only adds to the puzzle which they have for a long time presented to scholars.[16] They seem to have nothing in common, except that both fit into their periods of composition, about the middle of the first decade and the beginning of the second decade of the century. The more distinctive of the two, in its way a unique one, is the pattern of the play in regard to which Tourneur's authorship cannot be disputed, *The Atheist's Tragedy*. The closest parallel to the neatly rounded top of its graph, culminating at the fifth position and followed by high levels for the last two positions, is to be found in Jonson's *Alchemist*. Yet in nearly every other way Tourneur's verse here differs from Jonson's, especially in its avoidance of extra syllables and other noniambic metrical moves, except for truncated starts, and in the frequency of its almost foolhardy run-on procedures, more extreme even than Massinger's. Although the tragedy appeared only a year after the production of *The Alchemist*, in 1611, it seems difficult to assume any Jonsonian influence. Yet perhaps not altogether impossible: rhythmical influences work in subtle ways.

Another anomaly, of a somewhat earlier date, is the intriguing line-split design of Dekker's *Satiromastix*.[17] Dekker's emphasis on the iambic positions, which nearly always keeps him from practices resembling those of Massinger, putting him closer to Shakespeare, here appears in an unusual form—a design with three almost equally high peaks in the central stressed positions, like the teeth of a saw. No one iambic position dominates. He has been suspected of having received help from Marston in this play, and the only pattern of approximately the same period bearing any resemblance to it happens to be that of Marston's *Antonio and Mellida*.[18] There is more split-line thrust and parry of repartee and clash of series of abrupt short speeches in this play of Dekker's than anywhere else in his early

16. See p. 58.　　　17. See p. 53.　　　18. See p. 53.

work, recalling Marston's experimentation with the same devices in the second part of his first tragedy and in *Sophonisba*, and lending some support to those critics, including Chambers, who see Marston's hand in it.[19]

Dekker's career extends well into Caroline times, but his pause patterns keep most of their early characteristics, never adopting the typical features of the later part of the Jacobean era. Some younger playwrights, too, manage to keep unaffected by the trochaic fashion. Ford usually follows it, but Richard Brome's patterns look as though produced some fifteen to twenty years earlier.[20] Like those of Dekker and the late Fletcher, they seem to be following Shakespearean lines. This holds good also for some of Shirley's work.[21] His verse shows few signs of formal discipline, but in the matter of trochaic pauses he practises moderation. The question is whether this moderate attitude in his case, or that of Brome, is a sign of health. It looks rather as though what these writers were seeking was some easy middle way, some untroublesome, unadventurous routine. The time of heady enterprise had reached its end, experimentation was at an ebb, no strange, exciting rhythms stirred the blood. The new and daring things in poetry from now on were to happen outside of the drama.

The nadir of rhythmical shapelessness was soon to be reached in the plays of Sir William Davenant.[22] His sagging verse has little rhythmical life and less regularity. Yet here it is that the student of pause patterns meets with his greatest surprise. A look at the graph for his first play, *The Cruel Brother* (1627), almost makes one believe oneself to be back in the time before Marlowe. The wheel in this instance really has come full circle: it is not easy to distinguish this pattern from the first graph in our long series of line-split designs, that of Hughes' *Misfortunes of Arthur*. The iambic positions jut starkly up, the trochaic ones are down almost to zero, the fourth position reaches above the sixth. This familiar spiky design, with only minor modifications, reappears in quite a number of Davenant's later plays. The stout iambic pausal props seem to be needed to support the otherwise tumble-down structure of his degenerate verse.

19. E. K. Chambers, *The Elizabethan Stage*, III, 293.
20. See p. 59.   21. See p. 59.   22. See p. 59.

5. SOME SPECIAL APPLICATIONS
OF THE STUDY OF PAUSE
PATTERNS

In the preceding pages the focus has been on a narrow segment of the vast field of verse technique, but the phenomenon examined was of a sufficiently essential and symptomatic nature to take us into larger problems. Being isolated for intensive study in several hundred representative texts covering more than a century—an extraordinarily crowded century—it could be seen to be intimately connected with matters of far more obvious importance, some aspects of which it helped to illuminate. It was found to be expressive of the nature of periods as well as of personalities, of large movements as well as of much more strictly individual idiosyncrasies, even of literary relations between countries. An intensive method extensively applied helped to chart a wide area.

The same method can be used also for relatively minor points and puzzles. It should be possible to make use of it in approaching such matters, of vital concern to scholars, as problems of authorship and chronology, the customary purpose of studies in English Renaissance prosody. In a tentative way some suggestions relating to matters of this kind have already been made in the course of this paper, e.g. in respect to the chronology of *All's Well That Ends Well* or to the troublesome case of the authorship of *Henry VIII*.

Much caution is obviously needed, and the method must be developed to a point of greater refinement before conclusions in regard to such problems can be presented with any confidence. One might, for instance, have to examine the works in question section by section, act by act, even scene by scene, registering the data concerning different levels of pausal intensity, in order to discover the kinds and combinations of subpatterns and the ways in which they succeed one another and become modified in the course of a work. My own experiments, still unpublished, suggest that these patternings of patterns tend to differ in characteristic ways in different writers. Nothing useful can be achieved, however, unless the figures one works with are sufficiently high. Other handicaps are likewise numerous. The excessive prevalence of certain period patterns can make it impossible to find enough individuality of

30

design in a play or poem to indicate the author's identity. This is a difficulty one is up against in most early Tudor verse. Work written before an individual style is formed presents similar obstacles. Shakespeare's earliest patterns could easily have been produced by others, for example, by the author of *Arden of Feversham*, that distinctly non-Shakespearean play figuring so prominently among the Shakespeare Apocrypha.[1] What we see in it is a period pattern, not a pattern peculiar to any individual. *The Revenger's Tragedy*, often ascribed to Middleton rather than Tourneur, has a pattern not unlike that of Middleton's early *Phoenix* (whose authorship, however, has also been doubted), but there are several plays by other writers of that time whose pause arrangements it likewise resembles: it cannot be described as characteristically Middletonian.[2] All that can be stated is that such as it is the pause pattern does not contradict the assumption that Middleton wrote the play. What is perhaps even worse from the researcher's point of view than cases like those just described is the absence of any real guarantee that a writer with a well-defined pattern of his own will not deviate from it, if only once or twice in a long career. Even in Massinger such exceptional cases can be found. And if in an anonymous work or a work of dubious authorship one discovers what seems a pattern peculiar to a writer, one still had better look for additional evidence before committing oneself to a definite opinion. Two surprisingly similar patterns for which I have found no real parallels elsewhere stand side by side,[3] one of these the pattern of a play by Chapman, *All Fools*, the other that of a play of unknown authorship, *The Trial of Chivalry*, which nobody to my knowledge has as yet ventured to ascribe to Chapman, and probably nobody ever will.

Notwithstanding such snags and pitfalls of freakish coincidence and exceptional design, material of the kind here presented may serve as corroboratory evidence or may supply clues for further study. I have always been inclined to agree with most of Mr. F. L. Lucas's conclusions regarding different authors' shares in the more debatable plays included in his edition of Webster. My agreement has become firmer after an examination of the line-split patterns for these plays, which incidentally also support Mr. Lucas's chronological views. *Anything for a Quiet Life*, although reascribed to Middleton by W. D. Dunkel, in the parts attributed to Webster by Lucas has almost exactly the pattern of Webster's share in *The Fair Maid*

1. See pp. 42, 44.   2. See pp. 57, 58.   3. See p. 52.

of the Inn, to which it is near in time. *Appius and Virginia,* which Lucas places at the end of Webster's career, shows more resemblance to the pause pattern of the play after which it thus comes to stand, *A Cure for a Cuckold,* than to that of *The White Devil,* in whose neighborhood it has been supposed to belong. Although Heywood's part of it shows a pattern which occurs in his work intermittently at various times and consequently does not help Lucas's chronological case, while not damaging it, there is the further fact that if Lucas's attributions and chronology are accepted, Webster's line-split patterns are seen to evolve in a strikingly consistent and natural manner. In this instance the data concerning pauses seem to strengthen a case already strongly established by much weighty argument presented previously on very different grounds.

Another example of evidence weighting the balance in favor of conclusions reached before for different reasons, but still contested, is provided in our data concerning the authorship of *The Second Maiden's Tragedy.* Here the attribution of the play to Middleton, frequently made and as frequently attacked, would appear to receive considerable support from the extraordinary likeness of its line-split design to the mature patterns of Middleton, quite particularly in those plays closest to it in time, above all that of *The Witch.*

A matter of first importance, lying outside the dramatic field but not necessarily outside the scope of the method employed in this monograph, the problem of the relative chronology of the parts of the *Faerie Queene,* would deserve to be dealt with more fully from the point of view of pause structure. A theory concerning this matter was propounded not very long ago, partly on the basis of the punctuation of the poem, though not the punctuation of the original editors. The material I have collected appears to have some definite bearing on this problem, but its discussion must be reserved for a later occasion.

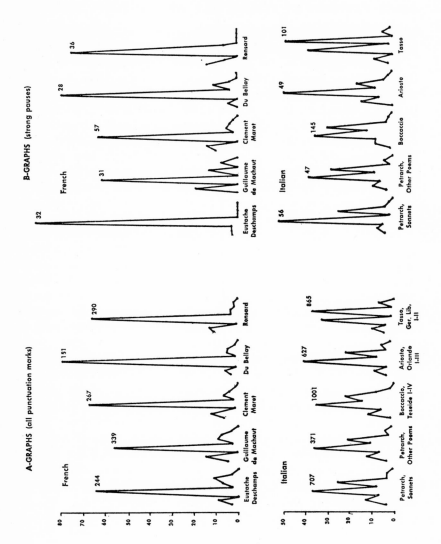

A-GRAPHS (all punctuation marks)

French

Eustache Deschamps 244
Guillaume de Machaut 339
Clement Marot 267
Du Bellay 151
Ronsard 290

Italian

Petrarch, Sonnets 707
Petrarch, Other Poems 371
Boccaccio, Teseide I-IV 1001
Ariosto, Orlando I-III 627
Tasso, Ger. Lib. I-II 865

B-GRAPHS (strong pauses)

French

Eustache Deschamps 32
Guillaume de Machaut 31
Clement Marot 57
Du Bellay 28
Ronsard 36

Italian

Petrarch, Sonnets 56
Petrarch, Other Poems 47
Boccaccio 145
Ariosto 49
Tasso 101

33

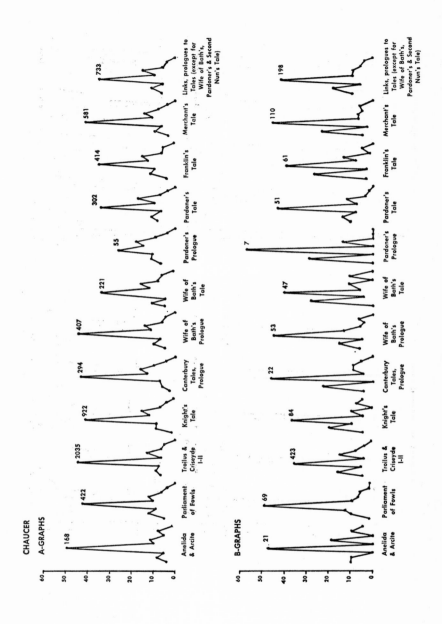

CHAUCER

A-GRAPHS

B-GRAPHS

34

A-GRAPHS

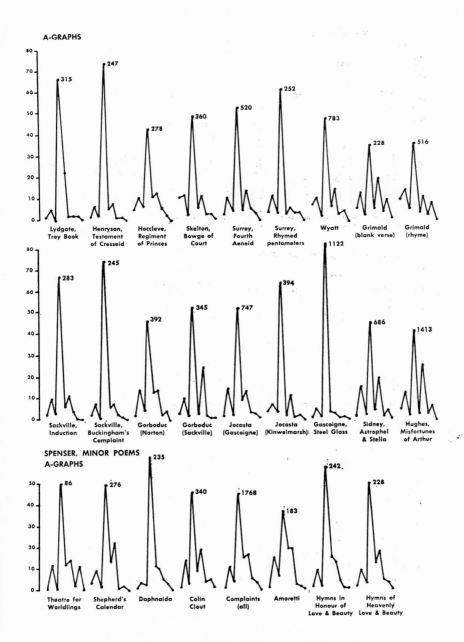

Lydgate, Troy Book — 315
Henryson, Testament of Cresseid — 247
Hoccleve, Regiment of Princes — 278
Skelton, Bowge of Court — 360
Surrey, Fourth Aeneid — 520
Surrey, Rhymed pentameters — 252
Wyatt — 783
Grimald (blank verse) — 228
Grimald (rhyme) — 516

Sackville, Induction — 283
Sackville, Buckingham's Complaint — 245
Gorboduc (Norton) — 392
Gorboduc (Sackville) — 345
Jocasta (Gascoigne) — 747
Jocasta (Kinwelmarsh) — 394
Gascoigne, Steel Glass — 1122
Sidney, Astrophel & Stella — 686
Hughes, Misfortunes of Arthur — 1413

SPENSER, MINOR POEMS A-GRAPHS

Theatre for Worldlings — 86
Shepherd's Calendar — 276
Daphnaïda — 235
Colin Clout — 340
Complaints (all) — 1768
Amoretti — 183
Hymns in Honour of Love & Beauty — 242
Hymns of Heavenly Love & Beauty — 228

35

SPENSER, MINOR POEMS
B-GRAPHS

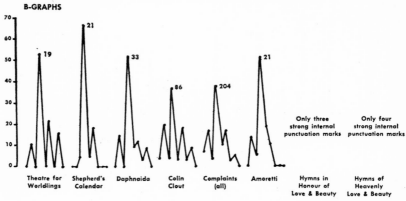

Theatre for Worldlings • Shepherd's Calendar • Daphnaida • Colin Clout • Complaints (all) • Amoretti • Only three strong internal punctuation marks — Hymns in Honour of Love & Beauty • Only four strong internal punctuation marks — Hymns of Heavenly Love & Beauty

SPENSER, FAERIE QUEENE (A-GRAPHS)

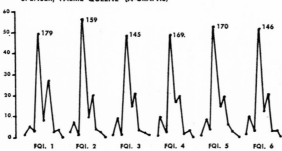

FQl. 1 • FQl. 2 • FQl. 3 • FQl. 4 • FQl. 5 • FQl. 6

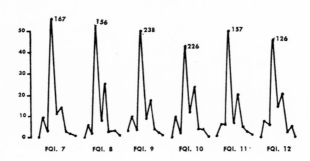

FQl. 7 • FQl. 8 • FQl. 9 • FQl. 10 • FQl. 11 • FQl. 12

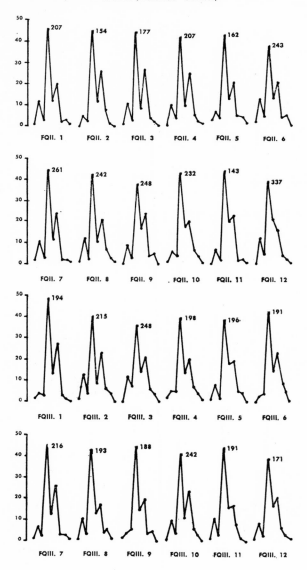

SPENSER, FAERIE QUEENE (A-GRAPHS - Continued)

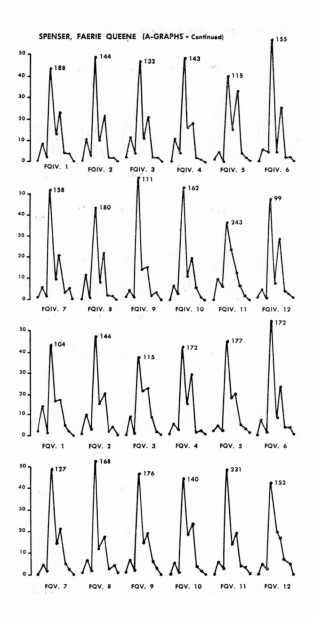

38

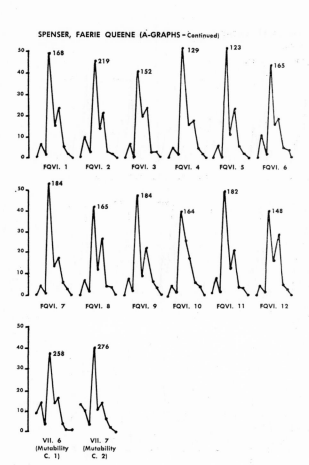

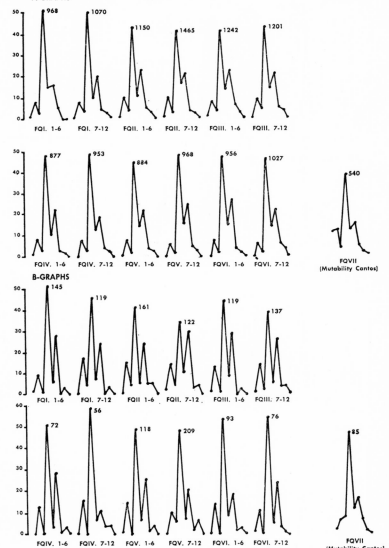

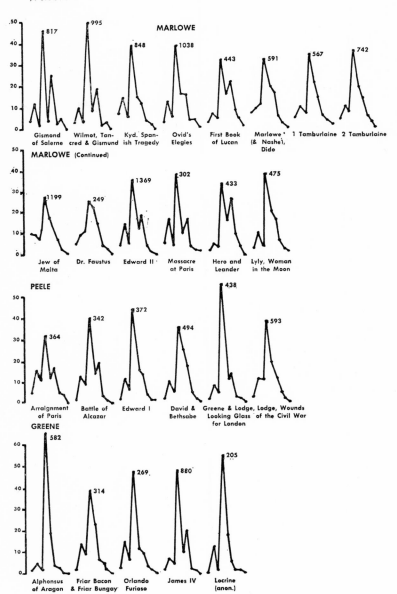

MARLOWE

Gismond of Salerne | Wilmot, Tancred & Gismund | Kyd, Spanish Tragedy | Ovid's Elegies | First Book of Lucan | Marlowe (& Nashe), Dido | 1 Tamburlaine | 2 Tamburlaine

817 | 995 | 848 | 1038 | 443 | 591 | 567 | 742

MARLOWE (Continued)

Jew of Malta | Dr. Faustus | Edward II | Massacre at Paris | Hero and Leander | Lyly, Woman in the Moon

1199 | 249 | 1369 | 302 | 433 | 475

PEELE

Arraignment of Paris | Battle of Alcazar | Edward I | David & Bethsabe | Greene & Lodge, Looking Glass for London | Lodge, Wounds of the Civil War

364 | 342 | 372 | 494 | 438 | 593

GREENE

Alphonsus of Aragon | Friar Bacon & Friar Bungay | Orlando Furioso | James IV | Locrine (anon.)

582 | 314 | 269 | 880 | 205

41

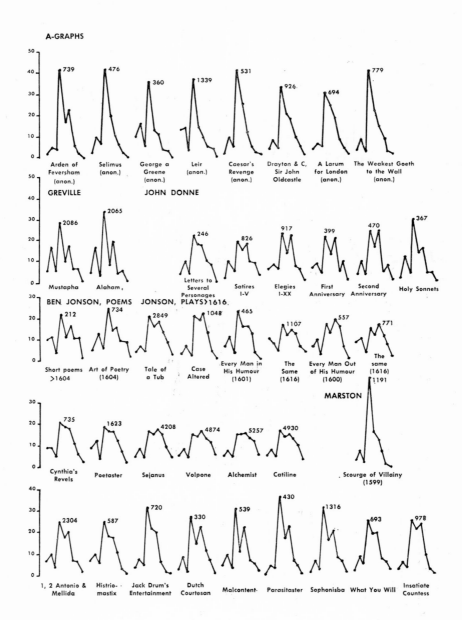

A-GRAPHS

| Arden of Feversham (anon.) | Selimus (anon.) | George a Greene (anon.) | Leir (anon.) | Caesar's Revenge (anon.) | Drayton & C, Sir John Oldcastle | A Larum for London (anon.) | The Weakest Goeth to the Wall (anon.) |

GREVILLE   JOHN DONNE

Mustapha   Alaham,   Letters to Several Personages   Satires I-V   Elegies I-XX   First Anniversary   Second Anniversary   Holy Sonnets

BEN JONSON, POEMS   JONSON, PLAYS >1616.

Short poems >1604   Art of Poetry (1604)   Tale of a Tub   Case Altered   Every Man in His Humour (1601)   The Same (1616)   Every Man Out of His Humour (1600)   The same (1616)

MARSTON

Cynthia's Revels   Poetaster   Sejanus   Volpone   Alchemist   Catiline   Scourge of Villainy (1599)

1, 2 Antonio & Mellida   Histrio-mastix   Jack Drum's Entertainment   Dutch Courtesan   Malcontent   Parasitaster   Sophonisba   What You Will   Insatiate Countess

42

B-GRAPHS (strong pauses)

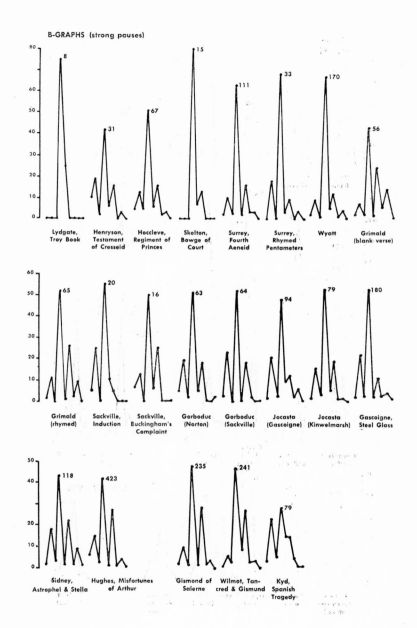

43

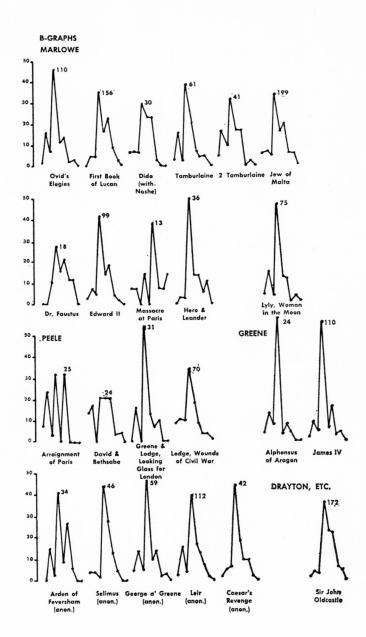

B-GRAPHS
MARLOWE

Ovid's Elagies — 110
First Book of Lucan — 156
Dido (with. Nashe) — 30
Tamburlaine — 61
2 Tamburlaine — 41
Jew of Malta — 199

Dr. Faustus — 18
Edward II — 99
Massacre at Paris — 13
Hero & Leander — 36
Lyly, Woman in the Moon — 75

PEELE

Arraignment of Paris — 25
David & Bethsabe — 24
Greene & Lodge, Looking Glass for London — 31
Lodge, Wounds of Civil War — 70

GREENE

Alphonsus of Aragon — 24
James IV — 110

Arden of Feversham (anon.) — 34
Selimus (anon.) — 46
George a' Greene (anon.) — 59
Leir (anon.) — 112
Caesar's Revenge (anon.) — 42

DRAYTON, ETC.

Sir John Oldcastle — 172

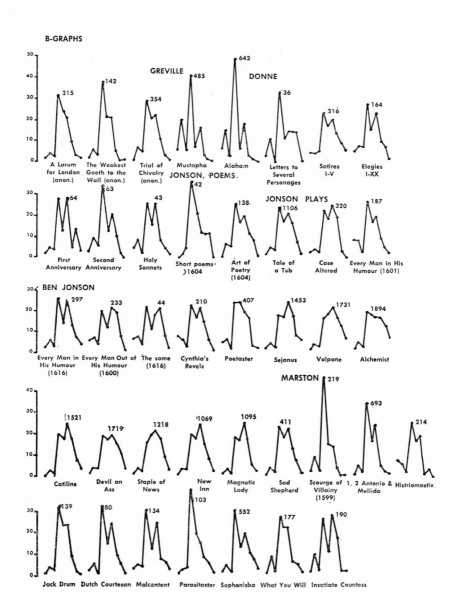

B-GRAPHS

GREVILLE DONNE

JONSON, POEMS.

JONSON PLAYS

BEN JONSON

MARSTON

45

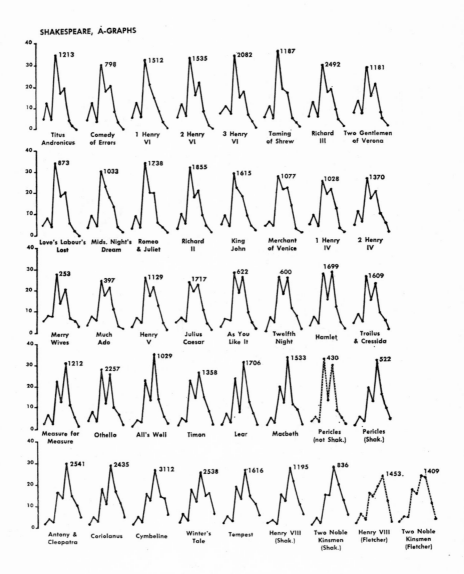

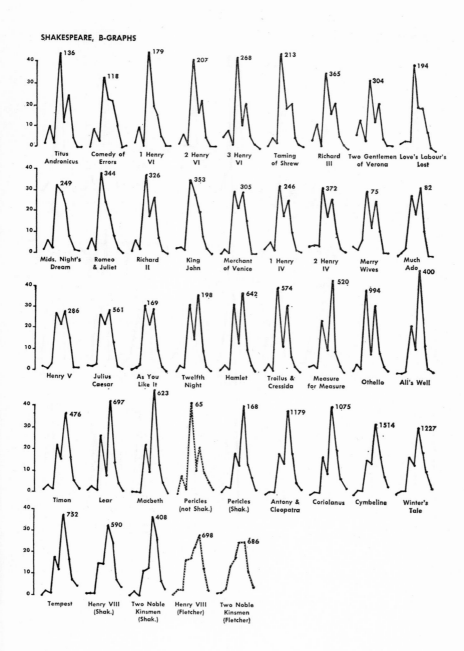

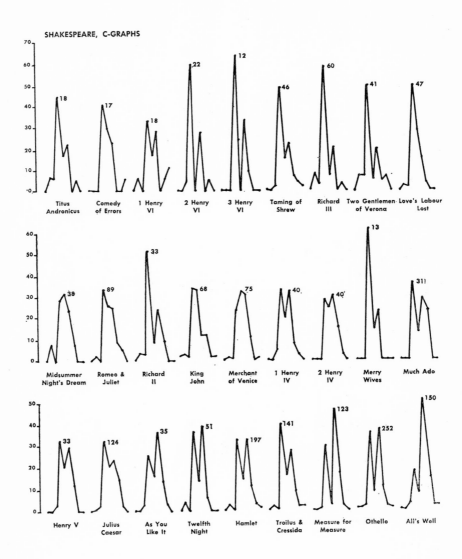

SHAKESPEARE, C-GRAPHS

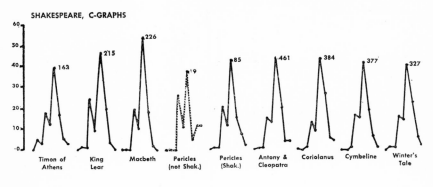

Timon of Athens — King Lear — Macbeth — Pericles (not Shak.) — Pericles (Shak.) — Antony & Cleopatra — Coriolanus — Cymbeline — Winter's Tale

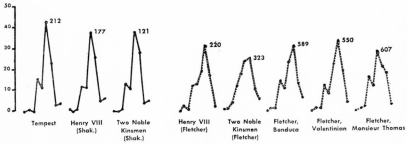

Tempest — Henry VIII (Shak.) — Two Noble Kinsmen (Shak.) — Henry VIII (Fletcher) — Two Noble Kinsmen (Fletcher) — Fletcher, Bonduca — Fletcher, Valentinian — Fletcher, Monsieur Thomas

SHAKESPEARE, RHYMED AND UNRHYMED PENTAMETERS
A-GRAPHS
POEMS   PLAYS

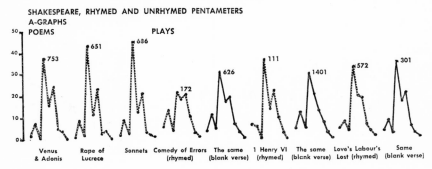

Venus & Adonis — Rape of Lucrece — Sonnets — Comedy of Errors (rhymed) — The same (blank verse) — 1 Henry VI (rhymed) — The same (blank verse) — Love's Labour's Lost (rhymed) — Same (blank verse)

49

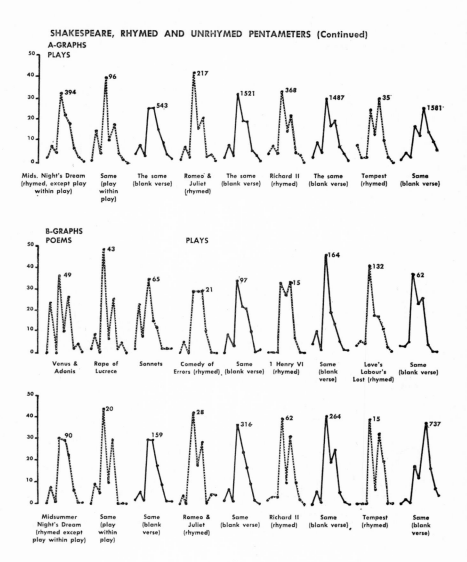

A-GRAPHS
PLAYS

Mids. Night's Dream (rhymed, except play within play) — 394
Same (play within play) — 96
The same (blank verse) — 543
Romeo & Juliet (rhymed) — 217
The same (blank verse) — 1521
Richard II (rhymed) — 368
The same (blank verse) — 1487
Tempest (rhymed) — 35
Same (blank verse) — 1581

B-GRAPHS
POEMS   PLAYS

Venus & Adonis — 49
Rape of Lucrece — 43
Sonnets — 65
Comedy of Errors (rhymed) — 21
Same (blank verse) — 97
1 Henry VI (rhymed) — 15
Same (blank verse) — 164
Love's Labour's Lost (rhymed) — 132
Same (blank verse) — 62

Midsummer Night's Dream (rhymed except play within play) — 90
Same (play within play) — 20
Same (blank verse) — 159
Romeo & Juliet (rhymed) — 28
Same (blank verse) — 316
Richard II (rhymed) — 62
Same (blank verse) — 264
Tempest (rhymed) — 15
Same (blank verse) — 737

50

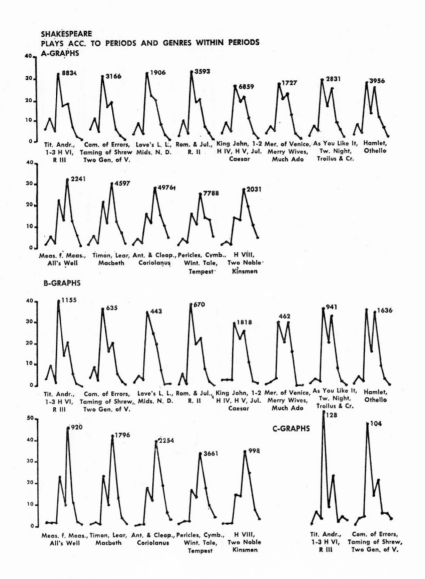

SHAKESPEARE
PLAYS ACC. TO PERIODS AND GENRES WITHIN PERIODS
A-GRAPHS

8834 3166 1906 3593 6859 1727 2831 3956

Tit. Andr., Com. of Errors, Love's L. L., Rom. & Jul., King John, 1-2 Mer. of Venice, As You Like It, Hamlet,
1-3 H VI, Taming of Shrew Mids. N. D. R. II H IV, H V, Jul. Merry Wives, Tw. Night, Othello
R III Two Gen. of V. Caesar Much Ado Troilus & Cr.

2241 4597 4976† 7788 2031

Meas. f. Meas., Timon, Lear, Ant. & Cleop., Pericles, Cymb.. H VIII,
All's Well Macbeth Coriolanus Wint. Tale, Two Noble ·
Tempest · Kinsmen

B-GRAPHS

1155 635 443 670 1818 462 941 1636

Tit. Andr., Com. of Errors, Love's L. L., Rom. & Jul., King John, 1-2 Mer. of Venice, As You Like It, Hamlet,
1-3 H VI, Taming of Shrew, Mids. N. D. R. II H IV, H V, Jul. Merry Wives, Tw. Night, Othello
R III Two Gen. of V. Caesar Much Ado Troilus & Cr.

920 1796 2254 3661 998 128 104

C-GRAPHS

Meas. f. Meas., Timon, Lear, Ant. & Cleop., Pericles, Cymb., H VIII,   Tit. Andr., Com. of Errors,
All's Well Macbeth Coriolanus Wint. Tale, Two Noble   1-3 H VI, Taming of Shrew,
Tempest Kinsmen   R III Two Gen. of V.

51

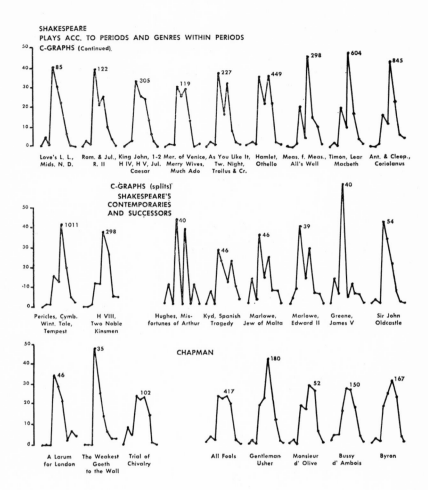

SHAKESPEARE
PLAYS ACC. TO PERIODS AND GENRES WITHIN PERIODS
C-GRAPHS (Continued).

C-GRAPHS (splits)
SHAKESPEARE'S
CONTEMPORARIES
AND SUCCESSORS

CHAPMAN

52

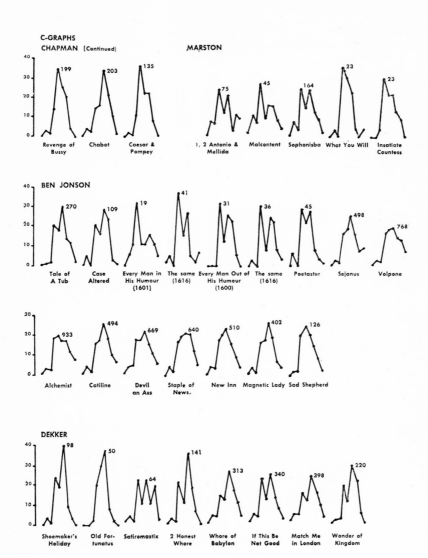

C-GRAPHS

CHAPMAN (Continued)

Revenge of Bussy — 199
Chabot — 203
Caesar & Pompey — 135

MARSTON

1, 2 Antonio & Mellida — 75
Malcontent — 45
Sophonisba — 164
What You Will — 23
Insatiate Countess — 23

BEN JONSON

Tale of A Tub — 270
Case Altered — 109
Every Man in His Humour (1601) — 19
The same (1616) — 41
Every Man Out of His Humour (1600) — 31
The same (1616) — 36
Poetaster — 45
Sejanus — 498
Volpone — 768

Alchemist — 933
Catiline — 494
Devil an Ass — 669
Staple of News — 640
New Inn — 510
Magnetic Lady — 402
Sad Shepherd — 126

DEKKER

Shoemaker's Holiday — 98
Old Fortunatus — 50
Satiromastix — 64
2 Honest Whore — 141
Whore of Babylon — 313
If This Be Not Good — 340
Match Me in London — 398
Wonder of Kingdom — 220

53

C-GRAPHS

DEKKER AS COLLABORATOR

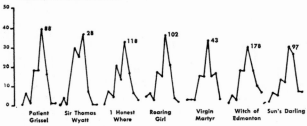

Patient Grissel — Sir Thomas Wyatt — 1 Honest Whore — Roaring Girl — Virgin Martyr — Witch of Edmonton — Sun's Darling

DEKKER'S COLLABORATORS

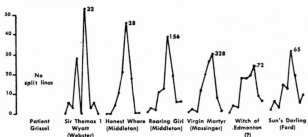

No split lines

Patient Grissel — Sir Thomas Wyatt (Webster) — 1 Honest Whore (Middleton) — Roaring Girl (Middleton) — Virgin Martyr (Massinger) — Witch of .Edmonton (?) — Sun's Darling (Ford)

HEYWOOD

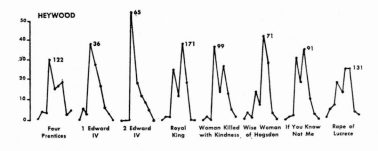

Four Prentices — 1 Edward IV — 2 Edward IV — Royal King — Woman Killed with Kindness — Wise Woman of Hogsdon — If You Know Not Me — Rape of Lucrece

54

HEYWOOD (Continued)

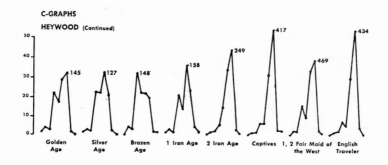

Golden Age · Silver Age · Brazen Age · 1 Iron Age · 2 Iron Age · Captives · 1, 2 Fair Maid of the West · English Traveler

145 · 127 · 148 · 158 · 249 · 417 · 469 · 434

JOHN DAY

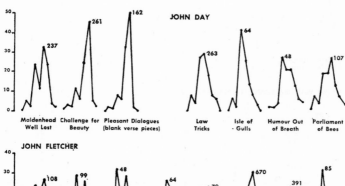

Maidenhead Well Lost · Challenge for Beauty · Pleasant Dialogues (blank verse pieces) · Law Tricks · Isle of Gulls · Humour Out of Breath · Parliament of Bees

237 · 261 · 162 · 263 · 64 · 48 · 107

JOHN FLETCHER

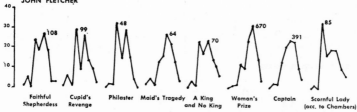

Faithful Shepherdess · Cupid's Revenge · Philaster · Maid's Tragedy · A King and No King · Woman's Prize · Captain · Scornful Lady (acc. to Chambers)

108 · 99 · 48 · 64 · 70 · 670 · 391 · 85

55

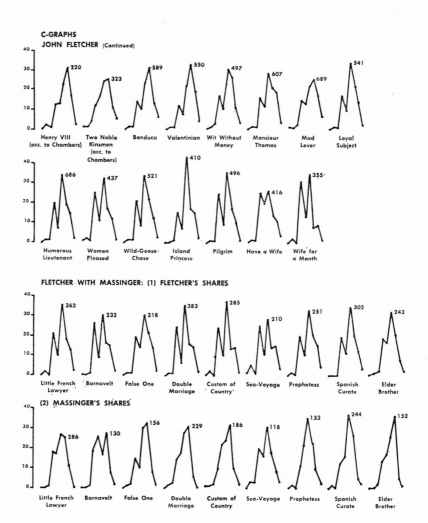

C-GRAPHS
JOHN FLETCHER (Continued)

Henry VIII (acc. to Chambers) — 220
Two Noble Kinsmen (acc. to Chambers) — 323
Bonduca — 589
Valentinian — 550
Wit Without Money — 497
Monsieur Thomas — 607
Mad Lover — 689
Loyal Subject — 541

Humorous Lieutenant — 686
Women Pleased — 437
Wild-Goose Chase — 521
Island Princess — 410
Pilgrim — 496
Have a Wife — 416
Wife for a Month — 355

FLETCHER WITH MASSINGER: (1) FLETCHER'S SHARES

Little French Lawyer — 362
Barnavelt — 232
False One — 218
Double Marriage — 383
Custom of Country — 285
Sea-Voyage — 210
Prophetess — 251
Spanish Curate — 302
Elder Brother — 242

(2) MASSINGER'S SHARES

Little French Lawyer — 286
Barnavelt — 130
False One — 156
Double Marriage — 229
Custom of Country — 186
Sea-Voyage — 118
Prophetess — 133
Spanish Curate — 244
Elder Brother — 152

56

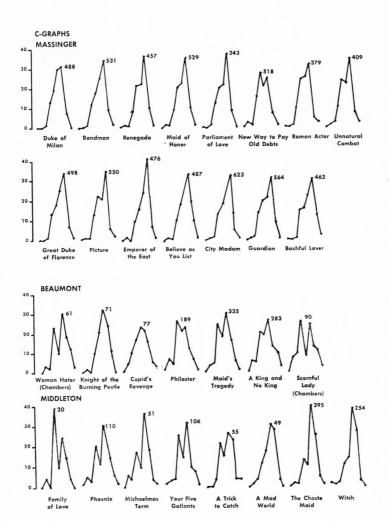

C-GRAPHS
MASSINGER

BEAUMONT

MIDDLETON

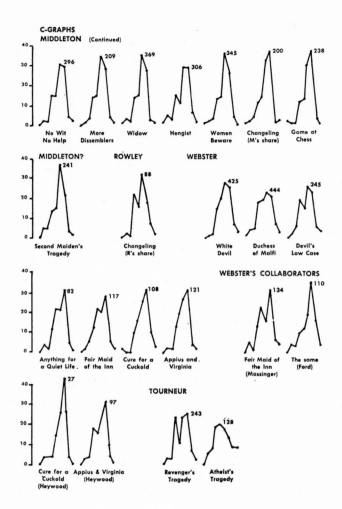

C-GRAPHS
MIDDLETON (Continued)

No Wit No Help — 296
More Dissemblers — 209
Widow — 369
Hengist — 306
Women Beware — 345
Changeling (M's share) — 200
Game at Chess — 238

MIDDLETON?   ROWLEY   WEBSTER

Second Maiden's Tragedy — 241
Changeling (R's share) — 88
White Devil — 425
Duchess of Malfi — 444
Devil's Law Case — 345

WEBSTER'S COLLABORATORS

Anything for a Quiet Life — 82
Fair Maid of the Inn — 117
Cure for a Cuckold — 108
Appius and Virginia — 121
Fair Maid of the Inn (Massinger) — 134
The same (Ford) — 110

TOURNEUR

Cure for a Cuckold (Heywood) — 27
Appius & Virginia (Heywood) — 97
Revenger's Tragedy — 243
Atheist's Tragedy — 128

58

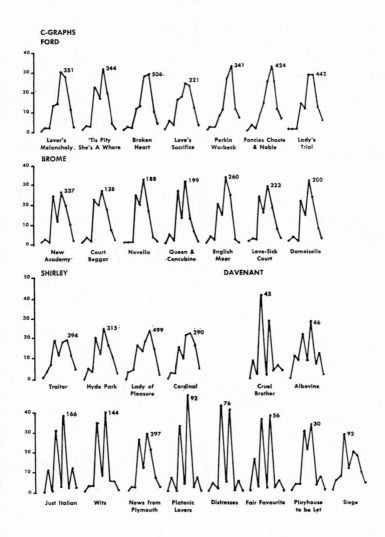

C-GRAPHS

FORD

- Lover's Melancholy — 351
- 'Tis Pity She's A Whore — 244
- Broken Heart — 506
- Love's Sacrifice — 221
- Perkin Warbeck — 341
- Fancies Chaste & Noble — 424
- Lady's Trial — 442

BROME

- New Academy — 337
- Court Beggar — 138
- Novella — 188
- Queen & Concubine — 199
- English Moor — 260
- Love-Sick Court — 323
- Damoiselle — 200

SHIRLEY

- Traitor — 394
- Hyde Park — 315
- Lady of Pleasure — 499
- Cardinal — 290
- Just Italian — 166
- Wits — 144
- News from Plymouth — 297
- Platonic Lovers — 92

DAVENANT

- Cruel Brother — 45
- Albovine — 46
- Distresses — 76
- Fair Favourite — 56
- Playhouse to be Let — 30
- Siege — 92

59

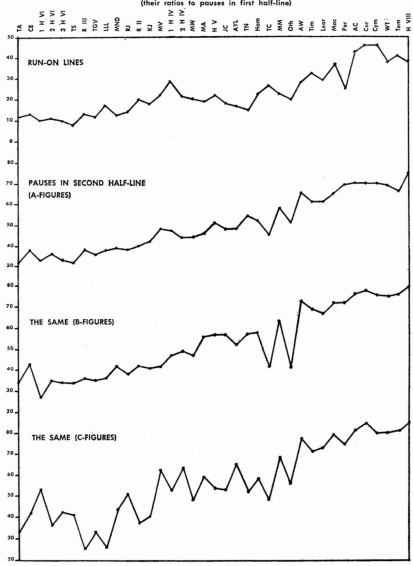

RUN-ON LINES AND PAUSES IN SECOND HALF-LINE
(their ratios to pauses in first half-line)

RUN-ON LINES

PAUSES IN SECOND HALF-LINE
(A-FIGURES)

THE SAME (B-FIGURES)

THE SAME (C-FIGURES)

60

A — FIGURES
(All internal punctuation marks)

TITLE	BASIC FIGURES										First Half	Even	PERCENTAGES								
	1	2	3	4	5	6	7	8	9	Total			1	2	3	4	5	6	7	8	9
Eustache Deschamps, Balades de moralites (first 30 pp.)	7	22	1	155	8	17	26	8	-	244	78.4	82.8	2.9	9.0	0.4	63.5	3.3	7.0	10.7	3.3	-
Guillaume de Machaut Jugement dou Roy de Behaingne (ll. 1-1000)	17	50	3	189	11	32	28	9	-	339	78.9	82.6	5.0	14.7	0.9	55.8	3.2	9.4	8.3	2.7	-
Clement Marot, Complaintes	19	32	3	179	4	16	11	3	-	267	88.6	86.1	7.1	12.0	1.1	67.0	1.5	6.0	4.1	1.1	-
Du Bellay, Antiquitez de Rome, Songe, Amours	5	9	1	119	1	8	7	1	-	151	89.3	90.7	3.3	6.0	0.7	78.8	0.7	5.3	4.6	0.7	-
Ronsard, Amours I. 1-30	32	37	4	189	8	8	7	5	-	290	92.9	82.4	11.0	12.8	1.4	65.2	2.8	2.8	2.4	1.7	-
Petrarch, Sonnets (Rime 1-200)	20	94	50	259	58	180	23	19	4	707	65.2	78.1	2.8	13.3	7.1	36.6	8.2	25.5	3.2	2.7	0.6
Petrarch, Other poems	16	46	26	135	41	79	11	13	4	371	64.3	76.3	4.3	12.4	7.0	36.4	11.1	21.3	2.9	3.5	1.1
Boccaccio, Teseide I-IV	15	116	60	350	138	218	80	20	4	1001	62.7	70.4	1.5	11.6	6.0	34.9	13.8	21.8	8.0	2.0	0.4
Ariosto, Orlando Furioso I-III	23	57	27	256	50	136	27	37	14	627	62.9	77.5	3.7	9.1	4.3	40.8	8.0	21.7	4.3	5.9	2.2
Tasso, Gerusalemme Liberata I-II	46	90	34	286	16	321	11	60	1	865	53.7	87.5	5.3	10.4	3.9	33.1	1.9	37.1	1.3	6.9	0.1
Chaucer, Anelida & Arcite	6	13	9	82	16	19	8	13	2	168	72.4	75.6	3.6	7.7	5.4	48.8	9.5	11.3	4.8	7.7	1.2
Parliament of Fowls	19	51	38	178	43	52	24	16	1	422	75.5	71.9	4.5	12.1	9.0	42.2	10.2	12.3	5.7	3.8	0.2
Troilus & Criseyde I-II	147	188	157	885	129	270	150	101	8	2035	72.2	71.4	7.2	9.2	7.7	43.5	6.3	13.3	7.4	5.0	0.4
Knight's Tale	22	87	85	378	113	135	62	33	7	922	70.7	68.1	2.4	9.4	9.2	41.0	12.3	14.6	6.7	3.6	0.8
Canterbury Tales, Prologue	8	17	20	126	38	46	28	11	-	294	66.8	67.5	2.7	5.8	6.8	42.9	12.9	15.6	9.5	3.7	-
Wife of Bath's Prologue	21	39	29	177	43	55	23	20	-	407	73.1	71.5	5.2	9.6	7.1	43.5	10.6	13.5	5.7	4.9	-
Wife of Bath's Tale	12	24	11	75	26	36	20	15	2	221	62.6	67.9	5.4	10.9	5.0	33.9	11.8	16.3	9.0	6.8	0.9
Pardoner's Prologue	4	6	6	14	8	10	5	2	-	55	63.8	58.2	7.3	10.9	10.9	25.5	14.5	18.2	9.1	3.6	-
Pardoner's Tale	28	34	21	103	31	50	21	13	1	302	68.6	66.3	9.3	11.3	6.9	34.1	10.3	16.6	6.9	4.3	0.3
Franklin's Tale	19	44	43	145	52	62	23	24	2	414	69.3	66.4	4.6	10.6	10.4	35.0	12.6	15.0	5.5	5.8	0.5
Merchant's Tale	25	56	41	237	67	82	48	24	1	581	69.8	77.6	4.3	9.6	7.1	40.8	11.5	14.1	8.3	4.1	0.2
Links, prologues to Tales (exc. Wife of Bath's, Pardoner's, Second Nun's Tales)	53	79	52	291	76	106	47	29	-	733	72.3	68.9	7.2	10.8	7.1	39.7	10.4	14.5	6.4	4.0	-

A — FIGURES (Continued)

Title	Basic Figures										First Half	Even	Percentages								
	1	2	3	4	5	6	7	8	9	Total			1	2	3	4	5	6	7	8	9
Lydgate, Troy Book I, 1-1028	3	16	1	207	73	5	5	5	-	315	96.7	74.0	1.0	5.1	0.3	65.7	23.2	1.6	1.6	1.6	-
Henryson, Testament of Cresseid	6	18	4	183	13	19	2	2	-	247	90.2	91.1	2.4	7.3	1.6	74.1	5.3	7.7	0.8	0.8	-
Hoccleve, Regiment of Princes, st. 1-75	13	31	19	119	34	37	16	9	-	278	74.6	74.2	4.7	11.2	6.8	42.8	12.2	13.3	5.8	3.2	-
Skelton, Bowge of Court	41	42	11	175	22	43	12	9	5	360	79.6	74.7	11.4	11.7	3.1	48.6	6.1	11.9	3.3	2.5	1.4
Surrey, 4th Aeneid	5	58	25	274	24	70	30	23	1	520	77.0	81.7	2.9	11.1	4.8	52.7	4.6	13.5	5.7	4.4	0.2
Surrey in Tottel's Misc. (all pentameters)	11	30	11	157	7	16	9	11	-	252	85.3	84.5	4.4	11.9	4.4	62.3	2.8	6.3	3.6	4.4	-
Wyatt in Tottel's Misc. (all pentameters)	59	82	22	379	58	120	22	41	-	783	83.2	79.4	7.5	10.5	2.8	48.4	7.4	15.3	2.8	5.2	-
Grimald in Tottel's Misc.																					
Blank verse	13	29	6	82	14	46	12	23	3	228	60.7	78.9	5.7	12.7	2.6	36.0	6.1	20.2	5.3	10.1	1.3
Rhymed pentameters	51	76	30	191	19	87	14	46	2	516	70.0	77.5	9.9	14.7	5.8	37.0	3.7	16.9	2.7	8.9	0.4
Sackville, Induction	4	24	4	155	14	25	6	1	-	233	85.4	88.0	1.7	10.3	1.7	66.5	6.0	10.7	2.6	0.4	-
Complaint of Buckingham	4	20	1	181	15	17	5	2	-	245	89.6	89.8	1.6	8.2	0.4	73.9	6.1	6.9	2.0	0.8	-
Gorboduc (Norton's share)	9	55	19	182	49	55	7	15	1	392	77.3	78.6	2.3	14.0	4.9	46.4	12.5	14.0	1.8	3.7	0.3
(Sackville's share)	9	35	6	184	11	87	7	4	2	345	70.1	89.9	2.6	10.1	1.7	53.3	3.2	25.2	2.0	1.2	0.6
Jocasta (Kinwelmarsh)	15	47	14	250	9	46	4	9	-	394	84.7	89.3	3.8	11.9	3.6	63.5	2.3	11.7	1.0	2.3	-
(Gascoigne)	18	113	16	391	64	94	24	22	5	747	78.8	83.0	2.4	15.1	2.1	52.3	8.6	12.6	3.2	2.9	0.7
Gascoigne, Steel Glass	6	54	16	934	44	35	16	14	3	1122	93.7	92.4	0.5	4.8	1.4	83.2	3.9	3.1	1.4	1.2	0.3
Sidney, Astrophel & Stella	16	111	23	315	37	134	11	34	5	686	71.7	86.6	2.3	16.2	3.4	45.9	5.4	19.5	1.6	5.0	0.7
Hughes, Misfortunes of Arthur	65	179	33	590	38	372	36	97	3	1413	63.1	87.6	4.6	12.7	2.3	41.8	2.7	26.3	2.5	6.9	0.2
Spenser, Faerie Queene (pentameters)																					
I. 1	2	9	6	88	14	48	5	7	-	179	63.6	84.9	1.1	5.0	3.4	49.2	7.8	26.8	2.8	3.9	-
2	3	11	1	89	13	31	7	4	-	159	70.3	85.0	1.9	6.9	0.6	56.0	8.2	19.5	4.4	2.5	-
3	1	13	3	69	20	30	5	3	1	145	68.8	79.3	0.7	9.0	2.1	47.6	13.8	20.7	3.4	2.1	0.7
4	-	15	4	83	29	32	1	5	-	169	72.9	79.8	-	8.9	4.9	49.1	17.2	18.9	0.6	3.0	-
5	1	13	6	89	16	32	8	5	-	170	70.8	81.8	0.6	7.6	3.5	52.4	9.4	18.8	4.7	2.9	-
6	1	13	5	74	22	24	7	-	-	146	75.0	76.0	0.7	8.9	3.4	50.7	15.1	16.4	4.8	-	-

62

This page contains a large statistical data table (rotated 90°). No column headers are printed on this page. The two leftmost columns are a group label (I., II., III.) and a sub-row label; the remaining 21 columns contain the data.

I.	1-6	8	74	25	492	114	197	33	24	1	968	70.1	81.3	0.9	7.6	2.6	50.8	11.8	20.4	3.4	2.5	0.1
I.	7	-	15	5	94	19	24	5	4	1	167	77.0	82.0	-	9.0	3.0	56.3	11.4	14.4	3.0	2.4	0.6
I.	8	-	9	3	84	12	39	5	4	1	156	66.7	87.2	-	5.8	1.9	53.8	7.7	25.0	2.6	2.6	0.7
I.	9	6	23	9	120	21	43	9	4	3	238	72.4	79.8	2.5	9.7	3.8	50.4	8.8	18.1	3.8	1.7	1.3
I.	10	1	23	4	98	27	55	10	8	1	226	63.3	81.4	0.4	10.2	1.8	43.4	11.9	24.3	4.4	3.5	-
I.	11	2	10	9	79	11	32	8	5	-	157	61.6	80.3	1.3	6.4	5.7	50.3	7.0	20.4	5.1	3.2	0.6
I.	12	-	10	7	58	17	25	3	6	-	126	68.8	78.6	-	7.9	5.5	46.0	13.5	19.8	2.4	4.8	-
I.	7-12	9	90	37	533	107	218	39	31	6	1070	73.2	81.5	0.8	8.4	3.5	49.8	10.0	20.4	3.6	2.0	0.6
II.	1	2	24	7	96	24	42	5	6	1	207	70.5	83.6	1.0	11.6	3.4	46.4	11.6	20.3	2.4	2.9	0.5
II.	2	-	8	5	69	18	40	12	2	-	154	60.3	77.3	-	5.2	3.2	44.9	11.6	26.0	7.8	1.3	-
II.	3	2	19	6	77	16	47	7	3	2	177	64.6	82.5	1.1	10.7	3.4	43.5	9.0	26.6	3.9	1.7	-
II.	4	1	20	9	86	21	52	11	5	2	207	62.4	78.7	0.5	9.7	4.3	41.5	10.1	25.1	5.3	2.4	1.0
II.	5	5	11	7	69	11	34	8	6	1	162	65.2	74.1	3.1	6.8	4.3	42.6	13.0	21.0	4.9	3.7	0.6
II.	6	4	31	12	93	31	50	9	13	-	243	66.0	77.0	1.6	12.8	4.9	38.3	12.8	20.6	3.7	5.3	-
II.	1-6	14	113	46	490	131	265	52	35	4	1150	65.1	78.4	1.2	9.8	4.0	42.6	11.4	23.0	4.5	3.0	0.4
II.	7	5	28	7	116	31	62	4	6	2	261	67.8	81.2	1.9	10.7	2.7	44.4	11.9	23.8	1.5	2.3	0.8
II.	8	2	29	5	102	27	50	18	7	2	242	64.2	77.7	0.8	12.0	2.1	42.1	11.2	20.7	7.4	2.9	0.8
II.	9	1	23	7	93	40	60	11	12	1	248	59.6	79.4	0.4	9.3	2.8	37.5	16.1	24.2	4.4	4.8	0.4
II.	10	2	14	9	101	42	46	13	7	2	232	65.6	71.8	0.9	6.0	3.8	43.2	18.0	19.7	5.5	3.0	-
II.	11	-	10	3	63	29	33	2	3	-	143	66.7	76.2	-	7.0	2.1	44.1	20.3	23.1	1.4	2.1	-
II.	12	1	39	18	131	72	55	13	7	1	337	71.3	68.8	0.3	11.6	5.3	38.9	21.4	16.3	3.8	2.1	0.3
II.	7-12	11	143	49	606	241	306	61	42	6	1465	66.1	74.9	0.7	9.7	3.4	41.4	16.5	20.9	4.2	2.9	0.4
III.	1	3	8	5	93	26	52	6	1	-	194	64.9	79.4	1.5	4.1	2.6	47.9	13.4	26.8	3.1	0.5	-
III.	2	2	28	9	85	19	50	13	9	-	215	63.3	80.0	0.9	13.0	4.2	39.5	8.8	23.3	6.0	4.2	-
III.	3	1	29	17	90	34	52	15	9	-	248	64.0	72.6	0.4	11.7	6.9	36.3	13.7	21.0	6.0	3.6	0.4
III.	4	3	29	9	77	27	50	13	7	1	198	57.9	72.7	1.5	5.1	4.5	38.9	13.6	25.3	6.6	3.5	1.0
III.	5	2	16	4	84	35	38	10	7	2	196	65.8	74.0	1.0	8.2	2.0	42.9	17.9	19.4	5.1	3.6	-
III.	6	-	6	8	80	27	44	17	9	-	191	57.3	72.8	-	3.1	4.2	41.9	14.1	23.0	8.9	4.7	-
III.	1-6	11	97	52	509	168	286	74	42	3	1242	62.3	75.2	0.9	7.8	4.2	41.0	13.5	23.0	6.0	3.4	0.2
III.	7	1	15	4	97	28	56	7	7	1	216	62.2	81.0	0.5	6.9	1.9	44.9	12.9	25.9	3.2	3.2	0.5
III.	8	2	21	12	83	25	35	7	11	1	193	67.9	77.7	1.0	10.9	4.1	43.0	12.9	18.2	3.6	5.7	0.5
III.	9	3	8	10	98	28	38	7	9	-	188	66.3	73.5	1.6	4.3	6.4	44.1	14.9	20.2	3.7	4.8	-
III.	10	3	24	10	92	27	59	14	6	1	242	62.8	73.8	1.2	9.9	4.1	40.5	11.2	24.4	5.8	2.5	0.4
III.	11	2	20	6	84	31	33	13	2	-	191	70.0	72.8	1.0	10.5	3.1	44.0	16.2	17.3	6.8	1.0	-

A — FIGURES (Continued)

TITLE	Basic Figures												Percentages								
	1	2	3	4	5	6	7	8	9	Total	First Half	Even	1	2	3	4	5	6	7	8	9
III. 12	2	16	5	67	29	36	10	5	1	171	63.4	72.5	1.2	9.4	2.9	39.2	17.0	21.1	5.8	2.9	0.6
7 12	13	104	45	512	168	257	58	40	4	1201	65.2	76.0	1.1	8.7	3.7	42.6	14.0	21.4	4.8	3.3	0.3
IV. 1	2	16	4	83	24	44	7	8	-	188	64.0	80.3	1.1	8.5	2.1	44.1	12.8	23.4	3.7	4.3	-
2	1	16	4	70	15	32	3	3	-	144	70.5	84.0	0.7	11.1	2.8	48.6	10.4	22.2	2.1	2.1	-
3	2	16	5	62	14	28	3	2	-	132	72.0	81.8	1.5	12.1	3.8	47.0	10.6	21.2	2.3	1.5	-
4	-	15	6	69	23	25	3	2	-	143	75.0	77.6	-	10.5	4.2	48.3	16.1	17.5	2.1	1.4	-
5	1	6	-	46	17	38	5	2	-	115	54.1	80.0	0.9	5.2	-	40.0	14.8	33.0	4.3	1.7	-
6	-	9	7	88	7	38	3	3	-	155	70.3	89.0	-	5.8	4.5	56.8	4.5	24.5	1.9	1.9	-
1-6	6	78	26	418	100	205	24	20	-	877	68.0	82.2	0.7	8.9	3.0	47.7	11.4	23.4	2.7	2.3	-
IV. 7	1	10	3	82	15	33	5	9	-	158	67.1	84.8	0.6	6.3	1.9	51.9	9.5	20.9	3.2	5.7	-
8	-	21	2	97	14	39	4	3	-	180	72.3	88.9	-	11.7	1.1	53.9	7.8	21.7	2.2	1.7	-
9	1	6	1	64	15	17	2	5	-	111	75.0	82.9	0.9	5.4	0.9	57.7	13.5	15.3	1.8	4.4	-
10	-	11	5	85	18	32	9	2	-	162	70.1	80.2	-	6.8	3.1	52.5	11.1	19.8	5.5	1.2	-
11	1	24	18	90	57	32	17	4	-	243	71.5	61.7	0.4	9.9	7.4	37.0	23.5	13.2	7.0	1.6	-
12	1	5	1	47	8	29	4	3	1	99	59.3	84.8	1.0	5.1	1.0	47.5	8.1	29.3	4.0	3.0	1.1
7-12	4	77	30	465	127	182	41	26	1	953	69.7	78.7	0.4	8.1	3.2	48.7	13.3	19.1	4.3	2.7	0.1
V. 1	2	14	1	45	17	18	5	2	-	104	62.1	76.0	1.9	13.5	1.0	43.3	16.3	17.3	4.8	1.9	-
2	-	14	4	68	21	29	3	5	-	144	69.9	80.6	-	9.7	2.8	47.2	14.6	20.2	2.1	3.5	-
3	-	10	1	43	24	25	10	2	-	115	59.3	69.6	-	8.7	0.9	37.4	20.9	21.7	8.7	1.7	-
4	2	11	4	73	26	50	2	3	1	172	62.3	79.6	1.1	6.4	2.3	42.4	15.1	29.1	1.1	1.7	0.6
5	3	9	5	80	31	36	8	5	-	177	65.6	73.4	1.7	5.1	2.8	45.2	17.5	20.3	4.5	2.8	-
6	-	13	1	92	14	39	7	6	-	172	67.1	87.2	-	7.6	0.6	53.3	8.1	22.6	4.1	3.5	-
1-6	7	71	16	401	133	197	35	23	1	884	65.9	78.3	0.9	7.9	1.8	45.4	15.0	22.4	4.0	2.6	0.1
V. 7	1	6	3	62	19	28	6	3	-	127	65.7	78.0	0.6	4.7	2.4	48.8	15.0	22.0	4.7	2.4	-
8	1	11	4	89	21	30	5	6	1	168	71.4	81.0	0.6	6.5	2.4	53.0	12.5	17.9	3.0	3.6	0.6
9	1	12	3	82	26	35	11	6	-	176	65.3	76.7	0.6	6.8	1.7	46.6	14.8	19.9	6.2	3.4	-
10	-	8	1	63	26	34	5	3	-	140	63.2	77.1	-	5.7	0.7	45.0	18.6	24.3	3.6	2.1	-
11	-	13	7	114	32	47	9	8	1	231	67.3	78.8	-	5.6	3.0	49.4	13.9	20.3	3.9	3.5	0.4
12	-	8	4	66	30	26	11	7	-	152	63.9	70.4	-	5.3	2.6	43.4	19.7	17.1	7.2	4.6	-

64

V. 7-12	2	58	22	476	154	200	47	33	2	994	66.4	77.2	0.2	5.8	2.2	47.9	15.5	20.1	4.7	3.3	0.2
VI. 1	1	12	3	83	25	41	1	2	-	168	69.2	82.1	0.6	7.1	1.8	49.4	14.9	24.4	0.6	1.2	-
2	2	22	6	101	31	46	6	5	-	219	69.7	79.5	0.9	10.0	2.7	46.1	14.2	21.0	2.7	2.3	-
3	-	11	2	63	30	36	5	4	1	152	62.3	75.0	-	7.2	1.3	41.4	19.7	23.7	3.3	2.6	0.7
4	-	7	3	67	21	23	6	2	-	129	71.3	76.7	-	5.4	2.3	51.9	16.3	17.8	4.7	1.5	-
5	-	7	-	64	14	29	7	2	-	123	65.1	82.9	-	5.7	-	52.0	11.4	23.6	5.7	1.6	-
6	-	18	3	72	26	31	8	7	-	165	66.9	77.6	-	10.9	1.8	43.6	15.8	18.8	4.8	4.2	-
VI. 1-6	3	77	17	450	147	206	33	22	1	956	67.5	79.0	0.3	9.1	1.8	47.1	15.4	21.5	3.5	2.3	0.1
VI. 7	-	10	4	98	25	33	11	6	-	184	68.6	79.9	-	5.4	0.5	53.3	13.6	17.9	6.0	3.3	-
8	1	12	6	69	20	45	8	6	-	165	59.3	80.0	0.6	7.3	2.4	41.8	12.1	27.3	4.9	3.6	-
9	-	15	3	87	16	42	13	8	-	184	62.5	82.6	-	8.2	1.6	47.3	8.7	22.8	7.1	4.3	-
10	-	8	3	66	42	28	10	7	-	164	63.1	66.5	-	4.9	1.8	40.2	25.6	17.1	6.1	4.3	-
11	1	14	4	89	21	38	8	7	-	182	67.1	81.3	0.5	7.7	2.2	48.8	11.5	20.9	4.4	3.8	-
12	-	7	3	59	24	43	8	4	-	148	55.6	76.4	-	4.7	2.0	39.9	16.2	29.1	5.4	2.7	-
VI. 7-12	2	66	18	468	148	229	58	38	-	1027	63.0	77.0	0.2	6.4	1.8	45.6	14.4	22.3	5.6	3.7	-
VII. 6	22	37	11	95	36	41	11	5	2	258	74.6	68.2	8.5	14.3	4.3	36.8	13.9	15.9	4.3	1.2	0.8
7	36	28	11	109	29	40	17	5	1	276	74.5	65.9	13.0	10.1	4.0	39.5	10.5	14.4	6.2	1.8	0.4
Spenser, Theatre for Worldlings		10	-	43	9	12	2	9	-	86	70.1	86.0	1.2	11.6	-	50.0	10.5	14.0	2.3	10.5	-
Shepherd's Calendar	7	24	6	135	35	60	3	6	-	276	71.4	81.5	2.5	8.7	2.2	48.9	12.7	21.7	1.1	2.2	-
Daphnaida	2	10	8	145	28	24	11	7	-	235	79.7	79.1	0.9	4.3	3.4	61.7	11.9	10.2	4.7	3.0	-
Colin Clout's Come Home	4	48	11	154	29	64	12	16	2	340	69.8	82.9	1.2	14.1	3.2	45.3	8.5	18.8	3.5	4.7	0.6
All poems in Complaints	25	188	72	795	272	277	81	53	5	1768	72.2	74.3	1.4	10.6	4.1	44.9	15.4	15.7	4.6	3.0	0.3
Amoretti	2	27	13	68	34	35	3	1	-	183	73.8	71.6	1.1	14.8	7.1	37.2	18.6	19.1	1.6	0.5	-
Hymns in Honor of Love & Beauty	2	22	3	138	37	30	9	1	-	242	80.5	78.9	0.8	9.1	1.2	57.0	15.3	12.4	3.7	0.4	-
Hymns of Heavenly Love & Beauty	1	21	6	114	28	42	9	6	1	228	71.0	80.3	0.4	9.2	2.6	50.0	12.3	18.4	3.9	2.6	0.4
Kyd, Spanish Tragedy	60	127	48	332	129	97	36	16	3	848	78.9	67.5	7.1	15.0	5.7	39.1	15.2	11.4	4.2	1.9	0.4
Marlowe, Dido	41	50	67	189	113	92	27	10	2	591	72.6	57.7	6.9	8.5	11.3	32.0	19.1	15.6	4.6	1.7	0.4
1. Tamburlaine	26	59	40	194	119	80	26	19	4	567	71.2	62.2	4.6	10.4	7.1	34.2	21.0	14.1	3.4	3.4	0.7
2. Tamburlaine	28	74	61	269	142	105	43	19	1	742	72.0	62.9	3.8	10.0	8.2	36.3	19.1	14.2	5.8	2.6	0.1
Jew of Malta	132	118	93	339	212	157	97	37	14	1199	69.1	54.3	11.1	9.7	7.8	28.3	17.7	13.1	8.0	3.1	1.1
Dr. Faustus	16	26	29	64	57	37	13	7	-	249	70.3	53.8	6.4	10.4	11.6	25.7	22.9	14.9	5.2	2.8	-
Edward II	63	211	84	486	182	259	62	19	2	1369	71.2	71.3	4.6	15.4	6.1	35.6	13.3	18.9	4.5	1.4	0.2
Massacre at Paris	17	51	16	117	30	50	11	5	5	302	73.9	73.8	5.6	16.9	5.3	38.7	9.9	16.6	3.6	1.7	1.7
Transl. of Ovid	30	136	63	400	163	163	36	45	2	1038	71.9	71.6	2.9	13.1	6.1	38.5	15.7	15.7	3.5	4.4	0.2

A — FIGURES (Continued)

Title	Basic Figures										First Half	Even	Percentages								
	1	2	3	4	5	6	7	8	9	Total			1	2	3	4	5	6	7	8	9
Transl, of Lucan	11	31	20	143	75	99	40	21	3	443	56.2	66.4	2.5	7.0	4.5	32.3	16.9	22.3	9.0	4.7	0.7
Hero & Leander	7	21	16	148	68	112	41	19	1	433	52.8	69.3	1.6	4.8	3.7	34.2	15.7	25.9	9.5	4.4	0.2
Wilmot, etc., Gismond of Salerne	29	96	17	372	30	207	25	41	-	817	65.3	87.6	3.5	11.8	2.1	45.5	3.7	25.3	3.1	5.0	-
Wilmot, Tancred & Gismund	27	101	41	494	91	184	23	32	2	995	73.3	81.5	2.7	10.2	4.1	49.6	9.2	18.5	2.3	3.2	0.2
Lyly, Woman in the Moon	15	48	21	181	95	75	28	9	3	475	69.6	65.9	3.2	10.1	4.4	38.1	20.0	15.8	5.9	1.9	0.6
Peele, Arraignment of Paris	17	53	40	117	43	63	17	13	1	364	70.7	67.6	4.7	14.6	11.0	32.1	11.8	17.3	4.7	3.6	0.3
Battle of Alcazar	7	45	30	137	47	64	9	3	-	342	74.2	72.8	2.0	13.2	8.8	40.1	13.7	18.7	2.6	0.9	-
Edward I	7	44	25	162	61	51	14	4	4	372	76.5	70.2	1.9	11.8	6.7	43.5	16.4	13.7	3.8	1.1	1.1
David & Bethsabe	8	48	23	177	121	83	23	11	-	494	68.6	65.0	1.6	9.7	4.7	35.8	24.5	16.8	4.7	2.2	-
Greene & Lodge, Looking Glass for London	8	37	20	244	48	62	11	7	1	438	79.2	79.9	1.8	8.4	4.6	56.0	11.0	14.2	2.5	1.6	0.2
Lodge, Wounds of Civil War	16	62	67	227	114	63	31	12	1	593	77.7	61.4	2.7	10.5	11.3	38.2	19.2	10.6	5.2	2.0	0.2
Greene, Alphonsus of Aragon	5	26	13	385	112	21	16	2	2	582	91.3	74.6	0.9	4.5	2.3	66.1	19.2	3.6	2.8	0.3	0.3
Friar Bacon & Friar Bungay	7	43	29	121	72	22	15	5	-	314	82.6	60.8	2.2	13.7	9.2	38.5	22.9	7.0	4.8	1.6	-
Orlando Furioso	9	41	18	130	31	26	10	4	-	269	83.2	74.7	3.4	15.2	6.7	48.3	11.5	9.7	3.7	1.5	-
James IV	14	61	41	434	97	187	30	15	1	880	70.2	79.2	1.6	6.9	4.7	49.3	11.0	21.2	3.4	1.7	0.1
Locrine	1	26	5	112	39	13	5	3	1	205	87.5	75.1	0.5	12.7	2.4	54.6	19.0	6.3	2.4	1.5	0.5
Arden of Feversham	16	39	29	307	123	168	45	12	-	739	63.5	71.2	2.2	5.3	3.9	41.5	16.6	22.8	6.1	1.5	-
Selimus	14	48	33	198	95	53	26	8	1	476	76.9	64.5	3.0	10.1	6.8	41.6	20.0	11.1	5.5	1.7	0.2
George a' Greene	37	57	23	128	47	40	15	12	1	360	78.3	65.8	10.3	15.8	6.4	35.6	13.0	11.1	4.2	3.3	0.3
Leir	178	184	57	490	187	117	68	53	5	1339	78.9	63.0	13.3	13.7	4.2	36.6	14.0	8.7	5.1	3.9	0.4
Caesar's Revenge	10	46	26	219	131	61	25	10	3	531	75.25	63.3	1.9	8.7	4.9	41.2	24.7	11.5	4.7	1.9	0.5
Sir John Oldcastle	32	76	32	306	186	160	81	45	8	926	60.3	63.4	3.5	8.2	3.5	33.0	20.1	17.3	8.7	4.9	0.9
Larum for London	26	43	35	210	165	126	56	25	8	694	59.3	58.2	3.7	6.2	5.0	30.3	23.8	18.2	8.1	3.6	1.2
Weakest Goeth to the Wall	21	61	25	311	165	108	65	17	6	779	68.1	62.5	2.7	7.8	3.2	40.0	21.2	13.9	8.3	2.2	0.8
Fulke Greville, Mustapha	127	347	126	606	216	377	133	132	22	2086	64.5	70.1	6.1	16.6	6.0	29.1	10.4	18.1	6.4	6.3	1.1
Alaham	101	354	79	701	183	407	98	118	24	2065	65.6	76.5	4.9	17.1	3.8	34.0	8.9	19.7	4.7	5.7	1.2
Donne, Storm, Calm, two poems to Sir H. Wotton	13	26	11	56	46	42	28	22	2	246	53.0	59.6	5.3	10.6	4.5	22.8	18.7	17.1	11.4	8.9	0.8

Satires I-V	28	91	51	162	132	155	92	84	31	826	59.6	47.8	3.4	11.0	6.2	19.6	16.0	18.9	11.1	10.2	3.7
Elegies I-XX	61	78	60	220	138	210	73	62	15	917	62.1	53.8	6.7	8.5	6.5	24.0	15.0	22.9	8.0	6.8	1.6
First Anniversary	30	40	18	93	57	87	23	44	7	399	66.2	52.9	7.5	10.0	4.5	23.3	14.3	21.8	5.8	11.0	1.8
Second Anniversary	25	52	23	116	63	115	27	41	8	470	63.1	53.1	5.3	11.1	4.9	24.7	13.4	24.5	5.7	8.7	1.7
Holy Sonnets	16	47	23	112	57	62	21	23	6	367	66.5	63.9	4.4	12.8	6.3	30.5	15.5	16.9	5.7	6.2	1.6
Jonson, Tale of Tub	146	208	139	602	469	543	387	261	94	2849	56.7	47.5	5.1	7.3	4.9	21.1	16.5	19.0	13.6	9.2	3.3
Case Is Altered	41	86	29	237	214	244	141	53	13	1048	58.2	45.9	3.9	8.2	2.8	21.7	20.4	23.3	13.5	5.1	1.2
Every Man in His Humour (1601)	36	55	17	111	80	79	64	17	6	465	56.3	56.9	7.7	11.8	3.7	23.9	17.2	17.0	13.8	3.7	1.3
(1616)	124	101	68	203	140	168	155	88	60	1107	50.6	51.5	11.2	9.1	6.1	18.3	12.6	15.2	14.0	8.0	5.4
Every Man Out of His Humour (1600)	43	59	22	100	80	110	92	38	13	557	55.1	47.0	7.7	10.6	3.9	18.0	14.4	19.7	16.5	6.8	2.3
(1616)	75	90	35	131	108	139	107	65	21	771	55.1	49.6	9.7	11.7	4.5	17.0	14.0	18.0	13.9	8.4	2.7
Cynthia's Revels	65	69	37	154	139	129	84	47	11	735	54.3	54.5	8.8	9.4	5.0	21.0	18.9	17.6	11.4	6.4	1.5
Poetaster	153	189	71	304	280	280	204	113	29	1623	54.6	53.4	9.4	11.6	4.4	18.7	17.2	17.2	12.6	7.0	1.8
Sejanus	221	388	199	719	651	767	635	439	189	4208	55.0	42.9	5.3	9.2	4.7	17.1	15.5	18.2	15.1	10.4	4.5
Volpone	300	415	231	754	752	832	694	593	301	4874	53.0	41.3	6.2	8.6	4.7	15.5	15.4	17.1	14.2	12.2	6.2
Alchemist	336	437	266	837	823	838	726	672	322	5257	53.0	42.3	6.4	8.3	5.1	15.9	15.7	15.9	13.8	12.8	6.1
Catiline	290	456	258	882	750	850	695	537	212	4930	55.3	45.1	5.9	9.2	5.2	17.9	15.2	17.2	14.1	10.9	4.3
Short poems dated up to 1604 by Herford and Simpson	22	23	8	47	26	37	24	23	2	212	61.3	53.8	10.4	10.8	3.8	22.3	12.3	17.5	11.3	10.8	0.9
Art of Poetry (1604)	37	92	43	180	108	116	75	68	15	734	62.1	56.2	5.0	12.5	5.9	24.5	14.7	15.8	10.2	9.3	2.0
Marston, 1-2 Antonio & Mellida	156	235	102	582	414	464	162	136	53	2304	61.5	56.9	6.8	10.2	4.4	25.3	18.0	20.1	7.0	5.9	2.3
Histriomastix	43	57	32	146	114	108	63	19	5	587	56.2	57.7	7.3	9.7	5.5	24.9	19.4	18.4	10.7	3.2	0.9
Jock Drum's Entertainment	29	58	35	230	155	144	51	13	3	720	62.3	61.8	4.0	8.1	4.9	31.9	21.5	20.0	7.1	1.8	0.7
Dutch Courtesan	9	28	8	92	49	76	41	24	3	330	66.7	48.8	2.7	8.5	2.4	27.9	14.8	23.0	12.4	7.3	0.9
Malcontent	27	55	22	169	59	125	38	34	10	539	71.1	56.9	5.0	10.2	4.1	31.4	10.9	23.2	7.1	6.3	1.8
Parasitaster	6	21	15	158	77	97	32	21		430	69.1	56.7	1.4	4.9	3.5	36.7	17.9	22.6	7.4	4.9	0.7
Sophonisba	32	91	43	419	206	282	124	88	31	1316	66.9	52.7	2.4	6.9	3.3	31.8	15.6	21.4	9.4	6.7	2.4
What You Will	20	65	38	183	138	136	56	38	19	693	60.9	55.1	2.9	9.4	5.5	26.4	19.9	19.6	8.2	5.5	2.7
Insatiate Countess	27	68	39	253	215	238	95	31	12	978	60.3	50.7	2.6	7.0	4.0	25.9	22.0	24.3	9.8	3.2	1.2
Scourge of Villainy (1599 ed.)	51	106	39	507	210	168	78	24	8	1191	67.6	70.6	4.3	8.9	3.3	42.6	17.6	14.1	6.5	2.0	0.7
Shakespeare, Titus Andronicus	60	141	65	429	208	234	57	18	1	1213	67.8	69.2	4.9	11.6	5.4	35.4	17.1	19.3	4.7	1.5	0.1
Comedy of Errors	35	97	34	236	145	160	63	25	3	798	64.9	61.6	4.4	12.2	4.3	29.6	18.2	20.1	7.9	3.1	0.4
1 Henry VI	80	184	71	480	307	208	127	50	5	1512	61.0	67.6	5.2	12.2	4.7	31.7	20.3	13.7	8.4	3.3	0.3
2 Henry VI	83	164	74	512	225	315	117	32	13	1535	66.6	63.6	5.4	10.7	4.8	33.4	14.7	20.5	7.6	2.1	0.8
3 Henry VI	138	205	143	713	309	351	149	71	3	2082	64.4	67.3	6.6	9.8	6.9	34.2	14.8	16.9	7.2	3.4	0.1

A — FIGURES (Continued)

Title	Basic Figures										First Half	Even	Percentages								
	1	2	3	4	5	6	7	8	9	Total			1	2	3	4	5	6	7	8	9
Taming of Shrew	63	117	52	422	228	206	58	33	8	1187	68.2	65.5	5.3	9.9	4.4	35.6	19.2	17.4	4.9	2.8	0.7
Richard III	138	310	122	715	434	457	186	110	20	2492	62.5	63.9	5.5	12.4	4.9	28.7	17.4	18.3	7.5	4.4	0.8
Two Gent. of Verona	97	141	79	328	174	230	78	42	12	1181	64.1	62.7	8.2	11.9	6.7	27.8	14.7	19.5	6.6	3.6	1.0
Love's Lab.'s Lost	42	70	31	296	167	173	56	30	8	873	62.2	65.2	4.8	8.0	3.6	33.9	19.1	19.8	6.4	3.4	0.9
Mids. Night's Dream	35	91	43	311	241	181	86	33	12	1033	60.6	59.6	3.4	8.8	4.2	30.1	23.3	17.5	8.3	3.2	1.2
Romeo & Juliet	44	159	65	597	346	341	104	63	19	1738	62.1	66.7	2.5	9.1	3.7	34.3	19.9	19.6	6.0	3.6	1.1
Richard II	61	183	91	585	326	383	133	79	14	1855	60.2	66.3	3.3	9.9	4.9	31.5	17.6	20.6	7.2	4.3	0.8
King John	80	148	58	464	338	295	141	66	25	1615	58.7	60.2	5.0	9.2	3.6	28.7	20.9	18.3	8.7	4.1	1.5
Merchant of Venice	39	67	43	289	230	235	140	24	10	1077	51.7	57.1	3.6	6.2	4.0	26.8	21.4	21.8	13.0	2.2	0.9
1 Henry IV	51	90	44	261	195	217	125	32	13	1028	53.5	58.4	5.0	8.8	4.3	25.4	19.0	21.1	12.2	3.1	1.3
2 Henry IV	60	149	82	351	226	271	133	80	18	1370	56.1	62.1	4.4	10.9	6.0	25.6	16.5	19.8	9.7	5.8	1.3
Merry Wives	14	20	19	69	36	54	18	15	8	253	56.2	62.5	5.5	7.9	7.5	27.3	14.2	21.3	7.1	5.9	3.2
Much Ado	17	32	25	101	73	87	43	12	7	397	54.0	58.4	4.3	8.1	6.3	25.4	18.4	21.9	10.8	3.0	1.8
Henry V	28	83	51	295	205	252	150	51	14	1129	49.4	60.3	2.5	7.4	4.5	26.1	18.2	22.3	13.3	4.5	1.2
Julius Caesar	77	115	106	417	337	396	184	64	21	1717	51.8	57.8	4.5	6.7	6.2	24.3	19.6	23.1	10.7	3.7	1.2
As You Like It	18	37	36	174	117	162	53	22	3	622	52.5	63.5	2.9	5.9	5.8	28.0	18.8	26.0	8.5	3.5	0.5
Twelfth Night	8	39	26	155	107	158	63	39	5	600	46.2	65.2	1.3	6.5	4.3	25.8	17.8	26.3	10.5	6.5	0.8
Hamlet	43	121	65	461	254	470	195	71	19	1699	47.8	66.1	2.5	7.1	3.8	27.1	14.9	27.7	11.5	4.2	1.1
Troilus & Cressida	61	125	67	496	237	375	145	81	22	1609	54.6	66.9	3.8	7.8	4.2	30.8	14.7	23.3	9.0	5.0	1.4
Measure for Measure	41	88	35	280	160	375	141	78	14	1212	42.2	67.7	3.4	7.3	2.9	23.1	13.2	30.9	11.6	6.4	1.2
Othello	82	181	86	633	260	577	235	158	45	2257	49.2	68.6	3.6	8.0	3.8	28.0	11.5	25.6	10.4	7.0	2.0
All's Well	9	36	27	232	147	357	146	57	18	1029	34.5	66.3	0.9	3.5	2.6	22.5	14.3	34.7	14.2	5.5	1.8
Timon	32	72	48	306	187	368	201	111	33	1358	39.1	63.1	2.4	5.3	3.5	22.5	13.8	27.1	14.8	8.2	2.4
King Lear	40	104	56	405	160	547	223	131	40	1706	39.1	69.6	2.3	6.1	3.3	23.7	9.4	32.1	13.1	7.7	2.3
Macbeth	36	82	46	313	181	523	179	139	34	1533	35.3	68.9	2.3	5.3	3.0	20.4	11.8	34.1	11.7	9.1	2.2
Pericles (non-S)	13	23	13	141	55	130	35	16	4	430	50.7	72.1	3.0	5.3	3.0	32.8	12.8	30.2	8.1	3.7	0.9
Pericles (S)	5	26	17	97	60	168	79	47	23	522	31.4	64.8	1.0	5.0	3.3	18.6	11.5	32.2	15.1	9.0	4.4
Antony & Cleopatra	40	108	72	428	352	752	390	274	125	2541	29.6	61.5	1.6	4.3	2.8	16.8	13.9	29.6	15.3	10.8	4.9
Coriolanus	37	112	70	429	259	699	413	284	132	2435	29.8	62.6	1.5	4.6	2.9	17.6	10.6	28.7	17.0	11.7	5.4
Cymbeline	61	159	104	493	389	796	473	445	192	3112	30.0	60.8	2.0	5.1	3.3	15.8	12.5	25.6	15.2	14.3	6.2
Winter's Tale	44	140	80	433	306	622	379	396	138	2538	31.2	62.7	1.7	5.5	3.2	17.1	12.1	24.5	14.9	15.6	5.4
Tempest	38	85	49	300	210	423	245	173	93	1616	33.6	60.7	2.4	5.3	3.0	18.6	13.0	26.2	15.2	10.7	5.8
Henry VIII (S)	25	34	26	177	157	328	246	131	71	1195	25.2	56.1	2.1	2.8	2.2	14.8	13.1	27.4	20.6	11.0	5.9
(Fletcher)	23	92	57	233	213	275	347	178	35	1453	32.6	53.5	1.6	6.3	3.9	16.0	14.7	18.9	23.9	12.3	2.4
Two Noble Kinsmen (S)	10	34	13	127	122	232	163	97	38	836	25.8	58.6	1.2	4.1	1.6	15.2	14.6	27.8	19.5	11.6	4.5
(Fletcher)	29	52	60	241	216	306	303	159	43	1409	32.0	53.8	2.1	3.7	4.3	17.1	15.3	21.7	21.5	11.3	3.1

Shakespeare's Plays According to Periods and Genres within Periods.

I. Histories, Tragedies: Titus And. 1-3 Henry VI, Rich. III	499	1004	475	2849	1483	1565	636	281	42	8834	65.7	64.5	5.6	11.3	5.4	32.3	16.8	17.7	7.2	3.2	0.5
II. Comedies: Comedy of Errors, Taming of Shrew, Two Gent. of Verona	195	355	165	986	547	596	199	100	23	3166	64.9	64.3	6.2	11.2	5.2	31.1	17.3	18.8	6.3	3.3	0.7
III. Lyrical Comedies: Love's Lab. Lost, Mids. Night's Dream	77	161	74	607	408	354	142	63	20	1906	61.3	62.2	4.0	8.5	3.9	31.8	21.4	18.6	7.5	3.3	1.0
IV. Lyrical Tragedy & History: Romeo & Juliet, Richard II	105	342	156	1182	672	724	237	142	33	3593	61.1	66.5	2.9	9.5	4.4	32.9	18.7	20.2	6.6	4.0	0.9
V. Histories, Tragedy: King John, 1-2 Henry IV, Henry V, Julius Caesar	296	585	341	1788	1301	1431	733	293	91	6859	54.2	59.7	4.3	8.5	5.0	26.1	19.0	20.6	10.7	4.3	1.3
VI. Comedies: Merchant of Venice, Merry Wives, Much Ado	70	119	87	459	339	376	201	51	25	1727	53.0	59.4	4.1	6.9	5.0	26.6	19.7	21.8	11.6	3.0	1.4
VII. Comedies: As You Like It, Twelfth Night, Troilus & Cressida	87	201	129	825	461	695	261	142	30	2831	52.4	65.8	3.1	7.1	4.5	29.2	16.3	24.6	9.2	5.0	1.1
VIII. Tragedies: Hamlet, Othello	125	302	151	1094	514	1047	430	229	64	3956	48.6	67.5	3.2	7.6	3.8	27.7	13.0	26.4	11.0	5.8	1.6
IX. Comedies: Measure for Measure, All's Well	50	124	62	512	307	732	287	135	32	2241	38.6	67.1	2.2	5.5	2.8	22.8	13.7	32.7	12.8	6.0	1.4
X. Tragedies: Timon, Lear, Macbeth	108	258	150	1024	528	1438	603	381	107	4597	37.6	67.5	2.4	5.6	3.2	22.3	11.5	31.3	13.1	8.3	2.3
XI. Tragedies: Antony & Cleopatra, Coriolanus	77	220	142	857	611	1451	803	558	257	4976	29.7	62.0	1.5	4.6	2.9	17.2	12.3	29.1	16.1	11.2	5.2
XII. Romances: Pericles (S), Cymbeline, Winter's Tale, Tempest	148	410	250	1323	965	2009	1176	1061	446	7788	31.2	61.7	1.9	5.3	3.2	16.9	12.4	25.8	15.1	13.6	5.7

A — FIGURES (Continued)

TITLE	BASIC FIGURES										First Half	Even	PERCENTAGES								
	1	2	3	4	5	6	7	8	9	Total			1	2	3	4	5	6	7	8	9
XIII. History & Tragicomedy: Henry VIII (S), Two Noble Kinsmen (S).	35	68	39	304	279	560	409	228	109	2031	25.4	57.1	1.7	3.3	1.9	15.0	13.7	27.6	20.1	11.2	5.4
Shakespeare, Poems																					
Venus & Adonis	12	59	10	289	118	193	39	30	3	753	58.3	75.8	1.6	7.8	1.3	38.4	15.7	25.6	5.2	4.0	0.4
Rape of Lucrece	5	59	15	285	85	153	21	27	1	651	64.3	80.5	0.8	9.0	2.3	43.8	13.1	23.6	3.2	4.1	0.2
Sonnets	14	61	17	312	90	154	20	14	4	686	67.8	78.9	2.0	8.9	2.5	45.5	13.1	22.4	2.9	2.0	0.6
Shakespeare, Rhymed Verse in Plays with Long Rhymed Passages																					
Comedy of Errors	10	24	6	38	32	36	19	5	2	172	55.7	59.9	5.8	14.0	3.5	22.1	18.6	20.9	11.0	2.9	1.2
1 Henry VI	8	7	-	41	16	25	11	3	1	111	58.9	68.5	7.2	6.3	-	36.9	14.4	22.5	9.9	2.7	-
Love's Lab. Lost	31	44	23	189	116	107	38	20	4	572	71.2	62.8	5.4	7.7	4.0	33.0	20.3	18.7	6.6	3.5	0.7
Mids. Night's Dream	9	45	20	170	101	94	34	14	3	490	69.7	65.9	1.8	9.2	4.1	34.7	20.6	19.2	6.9	2.9	0.6
Same (except play within in play)	8	30	15	131	90	76	29	12	3	394	60.5	63.2	2.0	7.6	3.8	33.2	22.8	19.3	7.4	3.0	0.8
Same (play within play)	1	15	5	39	11	18	5	2	-	96	70.6	77.1	1.0	15.6	5.2	40.6	11.5	18.75	5.2	2.1	-
Romeo & Juliet	4	17	7	93	36	45	6	8	1	217	66.8	75.1	1.8	7.8	3.2	42.9	16.6	20.7	2.8	3.7	0.5
Richard II	18	33	18	124	56	84	20	14	1	368	61.9	69.3	4.9	9.0	4.9	33.7	15.2	22.8	5.4	3.8	0.3
Tempest (masque in IV i)	3	1	1	9	5	11	4	1	-	35	46.7	62.9	8.6	2.9	2.9	25.7	14.3	31.4	11.4	2.9	-
Same Plays, Blank Verse																					
Comedy of Errors	25	73	28	198	113	124	44	20	1	626	63.4	66.3	4.0	11.7	4.5	31.6	18.0	19.8	7.0	3.2	0.2
1 Henry VI	72	177	71	439	291	183	116	47	5	1401	68.4	60.4	5.1	12.6	5.1	31.3	20.8	13.1	8.3	3.3	0.4
Love's Lab. Lost	11	26	8	107	51	66	18	10	4	301	60.8	69.5	3.7	8.6	2.7	35.5	16.9	21.9	6.0	3.3	1.3
Mids. Night's Dream	26	46	23	141	140	87	52	19	9	543	58.6	54.0	4.8	8.5	4.2	26.0	25.8	16.0	9.6	3.5	1.7
Romeo & Juliet	40	142	58	504	310	296	98	55	18	1521	61.4	65.5	2.6	9.3	3.8	33.1	20.4	19.5	6.4	3.6	1.2
Richard II	43	150	73	461	270	299	113	65	13	1487	59.8	65.6	2.9	10.1	4.9	31.0	18.2	20.1	7.6	4.4	0.9
Tempest	35	84	48	291	205	412	241	172	93	1581	33.3	60.7	2.2	5.3	3.0	18.4	13.0	26.1	15.2	10.9	5.8

B — FIGURES
(Strong pauses)

| TITLE | BASIC FIGURES | | | | | | | | | | | PERCENTAGES | | | | | | | | | |
	1	2	3	4	5	6	7	8	9	Total	First Half	Even	1	2	3	4	5	6	7	8	9
Eustache Deschamps, Balades de moralités (first 30 pp.)	1	1	1	29	-	-	-	-	-	32	100.0	93.75	3.13	3.13	3.13	90.6	-	-	-	-	-
Guillaume de Machaut, Jugement dou Roy de Behaingne 1-1000	-	6	-	19	-	4	-	2	-	31	80.6	100.0	-	19.3	-	61.3	-	12.9	-	6.5	-
Clement Marot, Complaintes	6	8	-	36	1	3	2	1	-	57	89.3	84.2	10.3	14.0	-	63.2	1.8	5.3	3.5	1.8	-
Du Bellay, Antiquitez de Rome, Songe, Amours	-	1	-	22	1	3	1	-	-	28	85.2	92.9	-	3.6	-	78.6	3.6	10.7	3.6	-	-
Pierre de Ronsard, Amours I 1-30	5	2	-	27	2	-	-	-	-	36	100.0	80.6	13.8	5.6	-	75.0	5.6	-	-	-	-
Petrarch, Sonnets (Rime 1-200)	2	4	3	29	1	14	2	1	-	56	69.1	85.7	3.6	7.1	5.4	51.8	1.8	25.0	3.6	1.8	-
Petrarch, Other poems	2	4	3	18	4	13	1	2	-	47	62.8	78.7	4.2	8.5	6.4	38.4	8.5	27.7	2.1	4.2	-
Boccaccio, Teseide I-IV	1	12	11	51	18	44	5	3	-	145	59.1	75.9	0.7	8.3	7.6	35.1	12.4	30.3	3.4	2.1	-
Ariosto, Orlando Furioso I-III	-	7	3	24	4	8	2	1	-	49	75.6	81.6	-	14.3	6.1	49.0	8.2	16.3	4.1	2.0	-
Tasso, Gerusalemme Liberata I-II	2	8	-	38	1	48	-	4	-	101	48.0	97.0	2.0	7.9	-	37.6	1.0	47.5	-	4.0	-
Chaucer, Anelida & Arcite	2	2	-	10	-	4	-	2	1	21	66.7	85.7	9.5	9.5	-	47.6	-	19.0	-	9.5	4.8
Parliament of Fowls	1	7	9	34	7	5	4	1	1	69	57.7	68.1	1.5	10.1	13.0	49.3	10.1	7.2	5.8	1.5	1.5
Troilus & Criseyde I-II	20	66	45	151	21	67	34	15	4	423	70.1	70.7	4.7	15.8	10.6	35.7	5.0	15.8	8.0	3.5	1.0
Knight's Tale	4	17	8	31	4	8	1	7	4	84	75.0	75.0	4.8	20.2	9.5	36.9	4.8	9.5	1.2	8.3	4.8
Canterbury Tales, Prologue	1	5	-	10	1	2	2	1	-	22	76.2	81.8	4.5	22.7	-	45.5	4.5	9.1	9.1	4.5	-
Wife of Bath's Prologue	3	8	3	24	7	3	2	3	-	53	82.6	71.7	5.7	15.1	5.7	45.3	13.2	5.7	3.8	5.7	-
Wife of Bath's Tale	-	13	2	19	3	5	-	5	-	47	77.3	89.4	-	27.7	4.3	40.4	6.4	10.6	-	10.6	-
Pardoner's Prologue	-	2	-	4	1	1	-	-	-	7	85.7	100.0	-	28.6	-	57.1	14.3	14.3	-	-	-
Pardoner's Tale	5	7	4	22	4	6	2	1	-	51	80.9	70.6	9.8	13.7	7.8	43.1	7.8	11.8	3.9	2.0	-
Franklin's Tale	2	16	2	24	5	8	1	3	-	61	78.6	83.4	3.3	26.2	3.3	39.3	8.2	13.1	1.6	4.9	-
Merchant's Tale	5	25	3	49	8	8	5	7	-	110	80.4	80.9	4.5	22.7	2.7	44.5	7.3	7.3	4.5	6.4	-

B — FIGURES (Continued)

Title	Basic Figures									9 Total	First Half	Percentages								
---	---	---	---	---	---	---	---	---	---	---	---	Even	1	2	3	4	5	6	7	8	9
	1	2	3	4	5	6	7	8	9												
Links, prologues in Canterbury Tales (exc. Wife of Bath's, Pardoner's, Second Nun's Tales)	19	35	11	81	18	17	9	8	-	198	81.1	71.2	9.6	17.7	5.5	40.9	9.1	8.6	4.5	4.0	-
Lydgate, Troy Book I, 1-1028	-	-	-	6	2	-	-	-	-	8	100.0	75.0	-	-	-	75.0	25.0	-	-	-	-
Henryson, Testament of Cresseid	3	6	1	13	2	5	-	1	-	31	79.3	77.4	9.7	19.4	3.2	41.9	6.4	16.1	-	3.2	-
Hoccleve, Regiment of Princes, st. 1-75	3	9	3	34	4	11	1	2	-	67	77.8	83.6	4.5	13.4	4.5	50.7	6.0	16.4	1.5	3.0	-
Skelton, Bowge of Court	-	-	-	12	1	2	-	-	-	15	85.7	93.3	-	-	-	80.0	6.7	13.3	-	-	-
Surrey, 4th Aeneid	2	11	2	70	2	18	3	3	-	111	78.0	99.0	1.8	9.9	1.8	63.1	1.8	16.2	2.7	2.7	-
Surrey in Tottel's Misc. (all pentameters)	-	6	-	22	1	3	-	1	-	33	87.5	97.0	-	18.2	-	66.7	3.0	9.1	-	3.0	-
Wyatt in Tottel's Misc. (all pentameters)	3	16	2	113	9	20	1	6	-	170	83.2	91.2	1.8	9.4	1.2	66.5	5.3	11.7	0.6	3.5	-
Grimald in Tottel's Misc. Blank verse	1	4	1	24	1	14	3	8	-	56	54.6	89.3	1.8	7.1	1.8	42.9	1.8	25.0	5.4	14.3	-
Rhymed pentameters	1	7	-	33	-	17	1	6	-	65	63.1	96.5	1.5	10.8	-	50.8	-	26.2	1.5	9.2	-
Sackville, Induction	1	5	-	11	2	1	-	-	-	20	94.2	85.0	5.0	25.0	-	55.0	10.0	5.0	-	-	-
Complaint of Buckingham	1	2	-	8	1	4	-	-	-	16	73.3	87.5	6.25	12.25	-	50.0	6.25	25.0	-	-	-
Gorboduc (Norton's share)	3	12	1	32	3	11	1	-	1	63	80.0	87.3	4.8	19.0	1.6	50.8	4.8	17.5	-	-	1.6
(Sackville's share)	2	15	-	33	-	13	1	-	-	64	78.1	95.3	3.1	23.4	-	51.6	-	20.3	1.6	-	-
Jocasta (Kinwelmarsh's share)	1	13	2	42	4	15	1	1	-	79	77.3	89.9	1.3	16.4	2.5	53.2	5.1	19.0	1.3	1.3	-
(Gascoigne's share)	2	19	1	45	8	11	2	6	-	94	77.9	86.2	2.1	20.2	1.1	47.8	8.5	11.7	2.1	6.4	-
Gascoigne, Steel Glass	3	40	5	95	4	19	5	7	2	180	81.25	89.4	1.7	22.2	2.8	52.8	2.2	10.5	2.8	3.9	1.1
Hughes, Misfortunes of Arthur	29	64	13	178	6	112	3	17	1	423	68.1	87.7	6.9	15.1	3.1	42.1	1.4	26.5	0.7	4.0	0.2
Sidney, Astrophel & Stella	2	21	4	51	1	26	1	11	1	118	66.7	92.4	1.7	17.8	3.4	43.2	0.8	22.0	0.8	9.3	0.8

Dense statistical table (rotated 90°). Column headers are not printed on this page; columns are numbered below for reference.

Work	1	2	3	4	5	6	7	8	9	10	11	12	13	14	15	16	17	18	19
Spenser, Faerie Queene,	2																	-	
I. 1 - 6	13	2	74	9	41	-	4	145	66.9	91.0	1.4	9.0	1.4	51.0	6.2	28.2	-	2.8	
I. 7 - 12	20	5	55	8	28	-	3	119	72.1	89.1	-	16.8	4.2	46.2	6.7	23.5	-	2.5	
II. 1 - 6	24	5	66	8	39	8	8	161	64.1	85.1	0.6	14.9	4.4	40.9	5.0	24.2	5.0	5.0	
II. 7 - 12	17	7	41	12	37	3	5	122	59.6	82.0	1.6	13.9	4.1	33.6	9.8	30.3	2.5	4.1	
III. 1 - 6	16	5	52	10	35	-	4	119	64.2	89.9	0.8	13.4	0.8	43.7	8.4	29.4	-	3.4	
III. 7 - 12	19	1	54	8	42	5	5	137	59.9	87.6	0.7	13.9	2.2	39.4	5.8	30.7	3.6	3.6	
IV. 1 - 6	9	3	37	2	21	1	2	72	65.7	95.8	-	12.5	-	51.4	2.8	29.2	1.4	2.8	
IV. 7 - 12	9	-	33	4	6	2	2	56	80.8	89.3	-	16.1	-	58.9	7.1	10.7	3.6	3.6	
V. 1 - 6	18	-	57	7	29	2	4	118	68.5	91.5	0.8	15.3	-	48.3	5.9	24.6	1.7	3.4	
V. 7 - 12	9	5	44	6	19	2	6	91	68.2	85.7	-	9.9	5.5	48.4	6.6	20.9	3.6	6.6	
VI. 1 - 6	13	-	49	8	18	2	3	93	72.9	89.2	-	14.0	-	52.7	8.6	19.4	2.2	3.2	
VI. 7 - 12	8	-	41	4	18	3	1	76	69.4	89.5	1.3	10.5	-	53.9	5.3	23.7	3.9	1.3	
Mutability cantos	5	7	40	10	14	6	1	85	72.0	70.6	2.3	5.9	8.2	47.2	11.7	16.5	7.1	1.2	
Spenser, Theatre for Worldlings	2	1	10	-	4	-	3	19	63.2	100.0	-	10.5	-	52.6	-	21.1	-	15.7	
Shepherd's Calendar	-	-	14	1	4	-	-	21	80.0	85.7	4.8	14.3	4.8	66.7	4.8	19.0	4.8	-	
Daphnaïda	5	1	17	3	4	1	3	33	73.3	87.9	15.2	15.2	-	51.5	9.1	12.1	3.0	9.1	
Colin Clout's Come Home	17	3	34	4	16	3	8	86	67.1	84.9	3.5	19.8	3.5	37.2	4.7	18.6	3.5	9.3	
All poems in Complaints	33	9	78	21	33	5	10	204	73.7	75.5	7.4	16.2	4.4	38.2	10.3	16.2	2.5	4.9	
Amoretti	3	1	11	4	2	1	1	21	88.2	76.2	-	14.3	4.8	52.4	19.0	9.5	4.8	2.5	1.3
Kyd, Spanish Tragedy	19	5	22	12	12	4	1	79	73.1	69.6	3.8	24.0	6.3	27.8	15.2	15.2	5.1	9.5	
Marlowe, Dido	2	2	9	7	7	-	1	30	65.2	60.0	6.7	6.7	6.7	30.0	23.3	23.3	3.3	3.3	
1 Tamburlaine	10	2	24	13	4	3	3	61	79.2	67.2	3.3	16.4	3.3	39.3	21.3	6.6	4.9	4.9	
2 Tamburlaine	7	4	13	7	7	1	1	41	68.3	68.3	4.9	17.1	9.8	31.7	17.1	17.1	2.4	2.4	
Jew of Malta	14	9	68	33	39	11	11	199	62.0	61.3	6.0	7.0	4.5	34.2	16.6	19.6	5.5	5.5	1.0
Dr. Faustus	-	2	5	3	4	2	2	18	46.7	61.1	3.0	8.1	11.1	27.8	16.7	22.2	5.1	11.1	
Edward II	8	5	42	15	19	5	-	99	69.0	71.7	7.7	7.7	5.1	42.4	15.1	19.2	7.7	11.1	
Massacre at Paris	1	-	2	-	5	1	2	13	30.8	69.2	3.0	-	-	15.4	-	38.5	7.7	2.0	15.4
Trans. of Ovid	17	8	50	13	15	2	1	110	79.4	77.3	7.7	8.1	7.3	45.5	11.8	13.6	9.6	2.7	
Trans. of Lucan	8	8	55	27	36	15	6	156	55.0	67.3	1.8	15.5	5.1	35.3	17.3	23.0	3.8	3.8	0.7
Hero and Leander	1	-	18	5	5	2	4	36	64.5	77.8	-	5.1	2.8	50.0	13.9	13.9	11.1	11.1	
Wilmot, etc., Gismond of Salerne	23	4	113	5	69	5	9	235	63.9	91.1	3.0	9.8	1.7	48.1	2.1	29.4	2.1	3.8	
Wilmot, Tancred & Gismund	7	-	17	4	2	-	3	31	81.5	77.4	-	16.1	-	54.8	12.9	6.5	9.7	-	
Lyly, Woman in the Moon	15	6	114	23	66	6	8	241	63.3	84.2	1.2	6.2	2.5	47.3	9.2	27.4	2.5	3.3	
Peele, Arraignment of Paris	11	3	35	10	9	1	3	75	80.0	77.3	4.0	14.7	4.0	46.7	13.3	12.0	1.3	3.3	
David & Bethsabe	6	1	8	-	8	-	-	25	68.0	88.0	8.0	24.0	4.0	32.0	-	32.0	-	4.0	
Greene & Lodge, Looking Glass for London	4	-	5	5	5	1	-	24	63.2	62.5	12.5	16.7	-	20.8	20.8	20.8	4.2	4.2	

B — FIGURES (Continued)

TITLE	BASIC FIGURES													PERCENTAGES								
	1	2	3	4	5	6	7	8	9	Total	First Half	Even	1	2	3	4	5	6	7	8	9
Lodge, Wounds of Civil War	6	7	7	24	13	6	3	3	1	70	77.2	57.1	8.6	10.0	10.0	34.3	18.6	8.6	4.3	4.3	1.4
Greene, Alphonsus of Aragon	1	3	2	14	1	2	1	-	-	24	87.9	79.2	4.2	12.5	8.3	58.3	4.2	8.3	4.2	-	-
Orlando Furioso	3	7	3	15	1	5	5	-	-	39	73.7	69.2	7.7	17.9	7.7	38.5	2.6	12.8	12.8	-	-
James IV	2	10	5	62	7	17	3	4	-	110	76.7	84.5	1.8	9.1	4.5	56.4	6.4	15.5	2.6	3.6	-
Arden of Feversham	-	5	1	14	3	9	2	-	-	34	64.5	82.4	-	14.8	2.9	41.2	8.8	26.5	5.9	-	-
Selimus	2	2	1	20	13	6	2	-	-	46	75.8	60.9	4.3	4.3	2.2	43.5	28.3	13.0	4.3	-	-
George a' Greene	3	8	3	28	8	6	1	2	-	59	79.2	78.0	5.1	13.6	5.1	47.4	13.6	10.2	1.7	3.4	-
Leir	3	18	4	45	19	14	7	2	-	112	75.3	70.5	2.7	16.1	3.6	40.2	17.0	12.5	6.2	1.8	-
Caesar's Revenge	1	2	3	19	8	4	4	1	-	42	73.5	61.9	2.4	4.8	7.1	45.2	19.0	9.5	9.5	2.4	-
Sir John Oldcastle	2	7	5	62	39	38	11	8	-	172	57.1	66.9	1.2	4.1	2.8	36.0	22.7	22.1	6.4	4.7	-
Larum for London	3	8	7	68	51	46	22	6	4	215	52.4	59.5	1.4	3.7	3.4	31.6	23.7	21.4	10.2	2.8	1.9
Weakest Goeth to the Wall	3	8	5	54	30	30	9	2	1	142	62.5	66.2	2.1	5.6	3.5	38.0	21.1	21.1	6.3	1.4	0.7
Trial of Chivalry	5	26	16	104	74	78	40	9	2	354	53.1	61.3	1.4	7.3	4.5	29.4	20.9	22.0	11.3	2.6	0.6
Fulke Greville, Mustapha	30	99	30	196	33	77	13	7	-	485	78.5	78.1	6.2	20.4	6.2	40.5	6.8	15.9	2.7	1.4	-
Alaham	40	94	16	312	37	117	18	7	1	642	76.4	82.6	6.2	14.6	2.5	48.6	5.8	18.2	2.8	1.1	0.2
Shakespeare, Titus Andronicus	2	14	3	60	16	34	7	-	-	136	65.8	79.4	1.5	10.3	2.2	44.1	11.8	25.0	5.1	-	-
Comedy of Errors	-	10	3	39	27	26	12	-	1	118	57.1	63.5	-	8.5	2.5	33.0	22.9	22.0	10.2	-	0.8
1 Henry VI	6	17	2	80	35	28	9	1	1	179	72.9	62.9	3.4	9.5	1.1	44.7	19.6	15.6	5.0	0.5	0.5
2 Henry VI	5	15	4	87	35	48	10	2	1	207	64.5	73.4	2.4	7.2	1.9	42.0	16.9	23.2	4.8	1.0	0.5
3 Henry VI	15	23	6	116	29	58	15	5	1	268	66.5	75.4	5.6	8.6	2.2	43.3	10.8	21.6	5.6	1.9	0.4
Taming of Shrew	3	10	6	95	40	42	11	4	2	213	65.9	70.9	1.4	4.7	2.8	44.6	18.8	19.7	5.2	1.9	0.9
Richard III	14	43	7	132	60	79	22	7	5	365	64.3	71.5	3.8	11.8	1.9	36.2	16.4	21.6	6.0	1.9	1.4
Two Gent. of Verona	20	41	12	100	38	67	15	6	5	304	65.0	70.4	6.6	13.5	3.9	32.9	12.5	22.0	4.9	2.0	1.6
Love's Lab. Lost	6	8	8	77	38	38	17	2	-	194	63.5	64.4	3.1	4.1	4.1	39.7	19.6	19.6	8.8	1.0	-
Mids. Night's Dream	3	16	5	79	71	51	20	2	2	249	57.9	59.5	1.2	6.4	2.0	31.7	28.5	20.5	8.0	0.8	0.8
Romeo & Juliet	7	23	4	129	81	63	28	8	1	344	62.0	64.8	2.0	6.7	1.2	37.5	23.5	18.3	8.1	2.3	0.3
Richard II	2	19	4	130	56	89	22	3	-	326	57.8	74.0	0.6	5.8	1.2	39.9	17.2	27.3	6.7	0.9	-
King John	10	12	8	123	67	69	27	6	1	353	59.8	59.5	2.8	3.4	2.3	34.8	19.0	19.5	7.6	1.7	0.3
Merchant of Venice	-	5	4	91	44	90	48	3	-	305	58.0	64.3	-	1.7	1.3	29.8	14.4	29.5	15.7	1.0	-
1 Henry IV	7	14	4	82	44	65	27	3	-	246	53.0	66.7	2.8	5.7	1.6	33.3	17.9	26.4	11.0	1.2	-
2 Henry IV	14	14	12	115	65	102	37	10	3	372	50.5	64.8	3.7	3.7	3.5	30.9	17.5	27.4	9.9	2.6	0.8

Merry Wives	3	2	6	23	10	20	9	1	1	75	52.3	61.3	4.0	2.7	8.0	30.7	13.3	26.6	12.0	1.3	1.3
Much Ado	-	2	3	24	16	27	10	-	2	82	43.9	64.6		2.4	3.7	29.3	19.5	32.9	12.2		1.3
Henry V	6	4	10	77	63	79	43	2	3	286	43.5	56.6	2.1	1.4	3.5	26.8	22.0	27.6	15.0	0.7	0.7
Julius Caesar	9	13	15	152	123	161	72	13	3	561	43.1	60.4	1.6	2.3	2.7	27.1	21.9	28.7	12.8	2.3	0.5
As You Like It	1	4	5	53	37	50	16	3		169	47.7	65.1	0.6	2.4	2.9	31.4	21.9	29.5	9.5	1.8	
Twelfth Night		5	5	63	29	74	19	4		198	42.6	73.7		2.5	2.0	31.8	14.6	37.4	9.6	2.0	
Hamlet	5	19	9	203	81	243	65	16	1	642	42.1	74.9	0.8	2.9	1.4	31.6	12.6	37.8	10.1	2.5	0.1
Troilus & Cressida	5	20	7	227	71	186	42	13	3	574	51.9	77.7	0.9	3.5	1.2	39.5	12.4	32.4	7.3	2.2	0.5
Measure for Measure	15	18	11	128	52	228	52	15	3	520	36.8	74.8	2.7	3.4	2.1	24.6	10.0	43.7	10.0	2.9	0.5
Othello	13	41	23	383	91	321	86	30	6	994	50.9	77.9	1.3	4.1	2.3	38.5	9.1	32.3	8.6	3.0	0.6
All's Well	-	1	3	91	45	197	53	6	4	400	26.8	73.7		0.2	0.7	22.7	11.2	49.2	13.2	1.5	1.0
Timon	4	13	7	103	70	176	74	23	6	476	31.3	66.2	0.8	2.7	1.5	21.6	14.7	37.0	15.5	4.8	1.3
King Lear	4	13	7	189	52	302	94	28	8	697	33.0	76.3	0.6	1.7	1.5	27.1	7.5	43.3	13.5	4.0	1.1
Macbeth	3	5	5	143	60	300	81	24	2	623	27.7	75.6	0.5	0.8	0.8	23.0	9.7	48.1	13.0	3.8	0.3
Pericles (S)	1	4	4	31	24	69	21	11	3	168	27.8	68.4	0.6	2.5	2.5	18.5	14.3	41.1	12.5	6.5	1.8
(non-S)	-	5	1	27	7	14	6	4	1	65	56.8	76.9				7.7	41.5	21.5	9.1	6.2	1.5
Antony & Cleopatra	3	10	13	220	160	466	222	59	28	1179	23.9	64.0	0.1	0.8	1.1	18.7	13.6	39.4	18.8	5.0	2.4
Coriolanus	6	8	15	189	99	436	215	74	36	1075	22.0	65.8	0.3	0.7	1.4	17.6	9.2	40.6	20.0	6.9	3.3
Cymbeline	10	30	29	242	224	506	273	140	64	1514	23.9	60.6	0.4	2.0	1.5	16.0	14.8	33.4	18.0	9.2	4.2
Winter's Tale	3	26	19	213	167	386	247	123	36	1227	25.3	60.7	0.4	2.1	0.9	18.2	12.2	31.5	20.1	9.9	2.9
Tempest	6	14	7	138	92	284	131	54	29	752	24.6	65.2	0.4	1.8	0.8	14.9	12.2	37.8	17.4	7.2	4.0
Henry VIII (S)	2	4	5	88	88	193	145	40	21	590	20.4	55.1	1.0	0.7	0.8	14.9	14.9	32.7	24.6	6.8	3.6
(Fletcher)	-	12	12	111	116	152	152	85	16	698	23.5	51.6	0.3	1.7	0.2	15.8	16.6	21.8	27.5	12.2	2.2
Two Noble Kinsmen (S)	-	7	1	48	51	153	107	28	13	408	15.7	57.8			0.2	11.8	12.5	37.5	26.2	6.9	3.2
(Fletcher)	6	8	21	95	116	168	170	77	25	686	22.8	50.7	0.9	1.2	3.1	13.8	16.9	24.5	24.7	11.2	3.6

Shakespeare's Plays according to Periods and Genres within Periods

I. Titus And., 1-3 Henry VI, Richard III	42	112	22	475	175	247	63	15	4	1155	64.6	73.5	3.5	9.7	1.9	41.1	15.1	21.4	5.5	1.3	0.3
II. Comedy of Errors, Taming of Shrew, Two Gent. of Verona	23	61	21	234	105	135	38	10	8	635	64.0	69.3	3.6	9.6	3.3	36.9	16.5	21.3	6.0	1.6	1.2
III. Love's Lab. Lost, Mids. Night's Dream	9	24	13	156	109	89	37	4	2	443	60.5	61.6	2.0	5.4	2.9	35.2	24.6	20.1	8.4	0.9	0.5
IV. Romeo & Juliet, Richard II	9	42	9	259	137	152	50	11	1	670	59.8	69.3	1.3	6.3	1.3	38.7	20.4	22.7	7.5	1.6	0.1
V. King John, 1-2, Henry IV. Henry V, Julius Caesar	46	57	49	549	392	476	206	34	9	1818	49.1	61.4	2.5	3.1	2.7	30.2	21.5	26.2	11.3	1.9	0.5

B — FIGURES (Continued)

Title	Basic Figures												Percentages								
	1	2	3	4	5	6	7	8	9	Total	First Half	Even	1	2	3	4	5	6	7	8	9
VI. Merchant of Venice, Merry Wives, Much Ado	3	9	13	138	93	137	67	1	1	462	44.2	61.7	0.6	1.9	2.8	29.9	20.1	29.7	14.5	0.2	0.2
VII. As You Like It, Twelfth Night, Troilus & Cressida	6	29	16	343	137	310	77	20	3	941	49.0	74.6	0.6	3.1	1.7	36.4	14.5	32.9	8.2	2.1	0.3
VIII. Hamlet, Othello	18	60	32	586	172	564	151	46	7	1636	47.5	76.8	1.1	3.7	2.0	35.8	10.5	34.5	9.2	2.8	0.4
IX. Measure for Measure, All's Well	15	19	14	219	97	425	105	21	5	920	32.4	74.3	1.6	2.0	1.5	23.8	10.5	46.2	11.4	2.3	0.5
X. Timon, Lear, Macbeth	11	31	19	435	182	778	249	75	16	1796	30.7	73.4	0.6	1.7	1.1	24.2	10.1	43.3	13.9	4.2	0.9
XI. Antony & Cleopatra, Coriolanus	4	18	28	409	259	902	437	133	64	2254	23.0	64.9	0.2	0.8	1.2	18.1	11.5	40.0	19.4	5.9	2.8
XII. Pericles (S), Cymbeline, Winter's Tale, Tempest	20	74	59	624	507	1245	672	328	132	3661	24.6	62.0	0.5	2.0	1.6	17.0	13.8	34.0	18.4	9.0	3.6
XIII. Henry VIII (S), Two Noble Kinsmen (S)	6	11	6	136	139	346	252	68	34	998	18.5	56.2	0.6	1.1	0.6	13.6	13.9	34.7	25.3	6.8	3.4
Shakespeare, Poems Venus & Adonis	-	10	-	18	5	13	1	2	-	49	63.6	87.7	-	20.4	-	36.7	10.2	26.5	2.0	4.1	-
Rape of Lucrece	1	4	-	21	3	11	1	2	-	43	65.0	86.4	2.3	9.3	-	48.8	7.0	25.6	2.3	4.7	-
Sonnets	1	15	5	23	10	8	1	1	1	65	80.0	72.3	1.5	23.1	7.7	35.4	15.3	12.4	1.5	1.5	1.5
Shakespeare, Rhymed Verse in Plays with Long Rhymed Passages Comedy of Errors	-	1	-	6	6	6	2	-	-	21	46.7	61.9	-	4.8	-	28.6	28.6	28.6	9.5	-	-
1 Henry VI	-	-	-	5	4	5	1	-	-	15	45.5	66.7	-	-	-	33.3	26.7	33.3	6.7	-	-
Love's Labour's Lost	4	6	5	54	24	22	15	2	-	132	63.9	63.6	3.0	4.5	3.8	40.9	18.2	16.7	11.4	1.5	-
Mids. Night's Dream	-	7	2	31	23	22	5	-	-	90	59.7	66.7	-	7.8	2.2	34.4	25.6	24.4	5.6	-	-
Same (except play within play)	-	5	1	22	21	16	5	-	-	70	57.1	61.4	-	7.1	1.4	31.4	30.0	22.9	7.1	-	-
Same (play within play)	-	2	1	9	2	6	-	-	-	20	66.7	85.0	-	10.0	5.0	45.0	10.0	30.0	-	-	-
Romeo & Juliet	-	1	-	12	5	8	-	1	1	28	56.5	78.6	-	3.6	-	42.9	17.9	28.6	-	3.6	3.6
Richard II	1	2	2	24	6	20	6	1	-	62	51.8	75.8	1.6	3.2	3.2	38.7	9.7	32.2	9.7	1.6	-

76

The following is a wide statistical table (rotated in the original). The row labels appear at the left; each row carries a set of count columns followed by a total and a set of percentage columns. Values shown as "·" are blank/dotted cells in the original.

	c1	c2	c3	c4	c5	c6	c7	c8	c9	Total	%	%	%	%	%	%	%	%	%	%	%	%
Tempest (Masque in IV. i.)	6	1	5	3	·	·	·	·	·	15	42.9	73.3	·	·	·	·	40.0	6.7	33.3	20.0	·	·
Same Plays, Blank Verse																						
Comedy of Errors	6	9	3	33	21	20	10	·	1	97	59.2	63.9	·	3.1	·	9.3	34.0	21.7	20.6	10.3	·	1.0
1 Henry VI	2	17	3	75	31	23	8	6	1	164	75.2	70.7	3.7	1.2	·	10.4	45.7	18.9	14.0	4.9	0.6	0.6
Love's Labour's Lost	3	2	3	23	16	16	2	2	·	62	62.5	66.1	3.2	3.2	·	3.2	37.1	22.6	25.8	3.2	·	·
Mids, Night's Dream	7	9	3	48	55	29	15	3	2	159	56.8	55.3	1.9	1.9	·	5.7	30.2	30.2	18.2	9.4	1.3	1.3
Romeo & Juliet	1	22	7	117	69	55	28	7	7	316	60.2	63.6	2.2	7.0	·	7.0	37.0	24.0	17.4	8.9	2.2	·
Richard II	3	17	4	106	50	69	16	2	2	264	59.3	73.5	0.4	0.9	·	6.4	40.2	18.9	26.1	6.1	0.8	·
Tempest	24	14	7	132	234	279	128	54	29	737	24.1	65.0	0.4	3.7	·	1.9	17.9	12.3	37.9	17.4	7.3	3.9
Jonson, Tale of a Tub	9	58	41	263	194	234	186	83	128	1106	42.3	55.3	2.2	3.4	·	5.2	23.8	17.5	21.2	16.8	7.5	2.1
Case Is Altered	16	13	11	74	80	80	61	10	1	320	41.3	55.3	2.8	2.7	·	4.1	23.1	19.1	25.0	19.1	3.1	0.3
Every Man in His Humour (1601)	8	16	10	51	37	49	18	9	4	187	56.4	56.0	8.5	3.0	·	8.5	27.3	16.6	19.8	9.6	4.8	2.1
(1616)	19	·	8	76	75	40	37	22	11	297	43.6	64.6	2.7	4.3	·	6.4	25.6	13.5	25.3	12.5	7.4	3.7
Every Man Out of His Humour (1600)	14	17	10	47	49	44	45	19	3	233	43.1	56.7	6.0	3.7	·	7.3	20.2	12.4	21.0	19.3	8.2	1.3
(1616)	14	15	8	48	40	30	46	18	3	216	44.0	56.0	6.5	3.3	·	6.9	22.2	10.6	18.5	21.3	8.3	1.9
Cynthia's Revels	16	13	7	99	78	66	30	13	6	210	48.3	56.2	7.6	2.0	·	6.2	24.4	23.6	21.0	14.3	6.2	1.4
Poetaster	19	23	8	96	66	78	66	12	6	407	47.9	52.1	4.6	2.3	·	5.7	18.3	17.0	19.2	16.2	2.9	1.5
Sejanus	29	53	34	266	247	357	257	117	93	1453	31.7	54.6	2.0	2.6	·	3.6	18.3	17.0	24.4	17.9	8.1	6.4
Volpone	35	71	46	276	310	356	294	231	112	1731	30.1	54.0	2.0	3.4	·	4.7	15.9	17.9	20.6	17.0	13.3	6.5
Alchemist	30	89	64	352	338	330	322	248	123	1894	36.7	53.7	1.6	2.2	·	3.0	18.6	18.1	17.4	17.0	13.1	6.5
Catiline	22	46	34	302	276	375	277	183	67	1521	32.5	55.5	1.4	4.3	·	4.4	19.9	18.4	24.7	18.2	8.0	4.4
Devil an Ass	31	76	74	328	316	338	272	127	101	1719	36.3	53.8	1.7	1.7	·	4.3	19.1	19.8	19.7	15.8	10.6	5.9
Staple of News	17	33	39	213	245	272	226	127	46	1218	31.0	52.9	1.4	3.1	·	4.4	17.2	18.4	22.0	18.3	10.3	3.7
New Inn	15	47	39	216	199	263	162	93	35	1069	36.4	57.9	1.4	3.6	·	3.9	20.2	18.6	24.6	15.1	8.7	3.3
Magnetic Lady	20	43	26	214	200	286	204	68	34	1095	33.9	55.8	1.8	2.4	·	4.6	19.4	18.3	26.1	18.6	6.3	3.1
Sad Shepherd	5	19	12	99	80	96	59	31	10	411	40.8	59.6	1.2	2.9	·	·	24.1	19.4	23.4	14.4	7.5	2.4
Short Poems Dated up to 1604 by Herford and Simpson	·	·	·	·	·	·	·	·	·	42	54.5	61.9	·	4.8	·	2.4	35.7	21.4	11.9	11.9	·	·
Art of Poetry (1604)	1	1	2	8	·	·	·	·	2	138	47.4	62.3	0.7	5.8	·	6.5	26.1	17.4	20.3	12.3	1.4	1.4
Donne, Storm, Calm, To Sir H. Wotton (2 poems)	1	9	·	12	·	4	·	·	·	36	53.1	72.2	2.8	·	·	11.1	33.3	11.1	13.9	13.9	·	·
Satires I-V	8	4	11	45	37	44	29	11	5	216	42.2	56.0	3.7	5.1	·	3.7	23.1	16.7	20.4	13.4	5.1	5.1
Elegies I-XX	8	8	2	50	18	37	14	3	29	164	54.0	63.4	4.9	6.7	·	6.7	27.4	15.2	22.6	8.5	6.7	1.2
First Anniversary	1	11	4	45	8	18	3	2	1	64	42.9	75.0	1.6	6.3	·	4.7	28.1	12.5	28.1	4.7	14.1	3.1
Second Anniversary	2	3	1	18	13	7	9	6	·	63	61.8	66.7	3.2	2.3	·	9.5	34.9	12.7	20.6	11.1	1.6	·
Holy Sonnets	2	6	1	11	7	11	4	1	2	43	50.0	65.1	4.7	·	·	9.3	25.6	16.2	25.6	9.3	2.3	2.3

B — FIGURES (*Continued*)

TITLE	BASIC FIGURES										First Half	Even	PERCENTAGES								
	1	2	3	4	5	6	7	8	9	Total			1	2	3	4	5	6	7	8	9
Marston, 1, 2 Antonio & Mellida	9	44	18	241	120	183	42	20	16	693	55.0	70.4	1.3	6.3	2.6	34.8	17.3	26.4	6.1	2.9	2.3
Histriomastix	17	12	7	56	36	43	35	8	-	214	51.7	55.6	7.9	5.6	3.3	26.2	16.8	20.1	1.7	3.7	-
Jack Drum's Entertainment	1	5	4	45	34	33	12	3	2	139	52.4	61.9	0.7	3.6	2.9	32.4	24.4	23.7	8.6	2.2	1.4
Dutch Courtesan	2	5	1	26	12	20	8	5	1	80	50.0	70.0	2.5	6.25	1.25	32.5	15.0	25.0	10.0	6.25	1.25
Malcontent	5	6	7	42	17	34	11	8	4	134	51.3	67.2	3.7	4.5	5.2	31.3	12.7	25.4	8.2	6.0	3.0
Parasitaster	1	3	4	42	21	16	9	6	1	103	61.0	65.0	1.0	2.9	3.9	40.8	20.4	15.6	8.7	5.8	1.0
Sophonisba	11	28	12	171	79	138	61	36	16	552	48.8	67.6	2.0	5.1	2.2	31.0	14.3	25.0	11.1	6.5	2.9
What You Will	2	15	4	50	41	40	12	9	4	177	52.2	64.4	1.1	8.5	2.3	28.2	23.2	22.6	6.8	5.1	2.3
Insatiate Countess	4	18	5	51	21	54	30	4	3	190	46.2	66.8	2.1	9.5	2.6	26.8	11.1	28.4	15.8	2.1	1.6
Scourge of Villainy (1599 ed.)	6	21	6	103	36	33	10	3	1	219	74.3	73.1	2.8	9.6	2.8	47.0	16.4	15.0	4.6	1.4	0.5

Title	Basic Figures										Percentages										
	1	2	3	4	5	6	7	8	9	Total	First Half	Even	1	2	3	4	5	6	7	8	9
Hughes, Misfortunes of Arthur	-	4	-	17	-	15	-	4	-	40	52.0	100.0	-	10.0	-	42.5	-	37.5	-	10.0	-
Kyd, Spanish Tragedy	-	3	-	13	10	5	10	4	1	46	44.4	54.4	-	6.5	-	28.3	21.7	10.9	21.7	8.7	2.2
Marlowe, Jew of Malta	-	6	1	16	6	11	3	3	-	46	57.5	78.3	-	13.0	2.2	34.8	13.0	23.9	6.5	6.5	-
Edward II	-	1	3	15	5	11	2	2	-	39	55.9	74.4	-	2.6	7.7	38.4	12.8	28.2	5.1	5.1	-
Greene, James IV	-	5	2	24	1	4	2	2	-	40	79.5	87.5	-	12.5	5.0	60.0	2.5	10.0	5.0	5.0	-
Sir John Oldcastle	-	1	-	22	17	11	3	-	-	54	62.2	63.0	-	1.9	-	40.7	31.5	20.4	5.5	-	-
Larum for London	-	-	-	16	14	10	1	3	2	46	50.0	63.0	-	-	-	34.8	30.4	21.7	2.2	6.5	4.3
Weakest Goeth to the Wall	-	-	-	17	9	5	2	1	1	35	65.4	65.7	-	-	-	48.6	25.7	14.3	5.7	2.9	2.9
Trial of Chivalry	-	9	5	25	23	24	15	1	-	102	49.4	57.8	-	8.8	4.9	24.5	22.6	23.5	14.7	1.0	-
Shakespeare																					
Titus Andronicus	-	1	1	8	3	4	-	1	-	18	66.7	77.8	-	5.5	5.5	44.4	16.7	22.2	-	5.5	-
Comedy of Errors	-	-	-	7	5	4	-	-	1	17	58.3	64.7	-	-	-	41.2	29.4	23.5	-	-	5.9
1 Henry VI	-	1	-	6	5	5	-	1	2	18	46.7	72.2	-	5.5	-	33.3	16.7	27.8	-	5.5	11.1
2 Henry VI	-	1	1	13	-	7	1	1	-	22	63.6	95.5	-	-	4.5	59.1	-	31.8	4.5	4.5	-
3 Henry VI	-	-	-	7	-	4	1	-	-	12	58.3	91.7	-	-	-	58.3	-	33.3	8.3	-	-
Taming of Shrew	-	-	1	22	7	10	3	2	1	46	59.0	73.9	-	-	2.2	47.8	15.2	21.7	6.5	4.3	2.2
Richard III	-	5	2	35	4	12	-	2	-	60	75.0	90.0	-	8.3	3.3	58.3	6.7	20.0	-	3.3	-
Two Gent. of Verona	-	3	3	20	2	8	2	3	-	41	66.7	82.9	-	7.3	7.3	48.8	4.9	19.5	4.9	7.3	-
Love's Lab. Lost	-	1	1	23	13	7	2	-	-	47	73.5	66.0	-	2.1	2.1	49.0	27.7	14.9	4.2	-	-
Mids. Night's Dream	-	3	-	11	12	9	3	-	-	38	53.8	60.3	-	7.9	-	28.9	31.6	23.7	7.9	-	-
Romeo & Juliet	-	2	-	30	23	22	8	4	-	89	48.5	65.2	-	2.2	-	33.7	25.8	24.7	9.0	4.5	-
Richard II	-	1	1	17	-	8	3	-	-	33	63.3	78.8	-	3.0	3.0	51.5	-	24.2	9.1	-	-
King John	1	2	1	23	23	8	8	1	1	68	60.0	50.0	1.5	2.9	1.5	33.8	33.8	11.8	11.8	1.5	1.5
Merchant of Venice	-	1	1	17	24	23	8	-	1	75	37.5	54.7	-	1.3	1.3	22.7	32.0	30.7	10.7	-	1.3
1 Henry IV	-	-	2	13	-	13	3	1	-	40	46.9	67.5	-	-	5.0	32.5	20.0	32.5	7.5	2.5	-
2 Henry IV	-	-	-	11	10	12	6	1	-	40	36.7	60.0	-	-	-	27.5	25.0	30.0	15.0	2.5	-
Merry Wives	-	-	-	8	2	3	-	-	-	13	61.5	84.6	-	-	-	61.5	15.4	23.1	-	-	-
Much Ado	-	-	-	11	4	9	7	-	-	31	40.7	64.5	-	-	-	35.5	12.9	29.0	22.6	-	-
Henry V	-	-	1	11	7	10	4	-	-	33	46.2	63.6	-	-	3.0	33.3	21.2	30.3	12.1	-	-
Julius Caesar	-	1	4	41	26	30	19	3	-	124	46.9	60.5	-	0.8	3.2	33.1	20.9	24.2	15.3	2.4	-
As You Like It	-	-	-	9	6	13	5	1	1	35	34.5	65.7	-	-	2.9	25.7	17.1	37.1	14.3	2.9	-
Twelfth Night	-	2	-	19	13	20	3	-	-	51	47.7	80.4	-	3.9	-	37.3	13.7	39.2	5.9	-	-
Hamlet	-	5	2	64	29	65	24	5	3	197	42.3	70.6	-	2.5	1.0	32.5	14.7	33.0	12.2	2.5	1.5

C — FIGURES (Continued)

TITLE	BASIC FIGURES										First Half	Even	PERCENTAGES								
	1	2	3	4	5	6	7	8	9	Total			1	2	3	4	5	6	7	8	9
Troilus & Cressida	-	3	1	57	24	39	11	3	3	141	52.1	72.6	-	2.1	0.7	40.4	17.0	27.7	7.8	2.1	2.1
Measure for Measure	-	-	1	37	4	58	21	2	3	123	31.9	78.9	-	-	0.8	30.1	3.2	47.2	17.1	1.6	-
Othello	3	3	4	91	22	94	27	5	-	252	43.9	76.6	1.2	1.2	1.6	36.2	8.7	37.3	10.7	2.0	1.2
All's Well	-	-	4	27	12	78	23	23	3	150	22.5	72.0	-	-	2.7	18.0	8.0	52.0	15.3	2.0	2.0
Timon	-	8	4	29	19	63	27	8	5	163	28.5	66.3	-	4.9	2.5	17.8	11.6	38.6	16.6	4.9	3.1
King Lear	-	1	-	51	17	99	40	6	-	215	26.8	73.0	-	0.5	0.5	23.7	8.0	46.0	18.6	2.8	-
Macbeth	-	-	1	43	22	120	37	4	2	226	21.1	73.9	-	-	-	19.0	9.7	53.1	16.3	1.8	-
Pericles (S.)	-	1	1	17	9	36	13	6	2	85	25.0	70.6	-	1.2	1.2	20.0	10.6	42.3	15.3	7.1	2.4
(Non S.)	-	-	-	5	2	7	1	2	2	19	29.4	73.7	-	-	-	26.3	10.5	36.8	5.3	10.5	10.5
Antony & Cleopatra	1	3	4	68	59	198	91	19	18	461	18.9	62.6	0.2	0.7	0.9	14.8	12.8	42.9	19.7	4.1	3.9
Coriolanus	-	1	2	48	35	164	99	20	15	384	14.6	60.7	-	0.3	0.5	12.5	9.1	42.7	25.8	5.2	3.9
Cymbeline	-	1	2	61	57	155	72	24	5	377	20.0	63.7	-	0.3	0.5	16.2	15.1	41.1	19.1	6.4	1.3
Winter's Tale	-	2	2	53	45	130	72	18	5	327	20.2	62.1	-	0.6	0.6	16.2	13.8	39.8	22.0	5.5	1.5
Tempest	-	2	-	34	23	90	49	6	8	212	19.0	62.3	-	0.9	-	16.0	10.8	42.5	23.1	2.8	3.8
Henry VIII (S.)	1	-	1	21	22	67	46	9	10	177	14.8	54.8	0.6	-	0.6	11.9	12.4	37.9	26.0	5.1	5.6
The Two Noble Kinsmen (S.)	-	-	1	16	13	46	34	5	6	121	15.7	55.4	-	-	0.8	13.2	10.7	38.1	28.1	4.1	5.0
Shakespeare's Plays Acc. to Periods and Genres within Periods																					
I. Titus Andr., 1-3 Henry VI, Rich. III	-	7	4	68	10	30	1	5	3	128	67.8	85.9	-	5.5	3.1	53.1	7.8	23.4	0.8	3.9	2.3
II. Com. of Errors, Taming of Shrew, Two Gent. of Verona	-	3	4	49	14	22	5	5	2	104	62.2	76.0	-	2.9	3.8	47.1	13.5	21.2	4.8	4.8	1.9
III. Love's Lab. Lost, Mids. N. Dream	-	4	1	34	25	16	5	-	-	85	55.7	63.5	-	4.7	1.2	40.0	29.4	18.8	5.9	-	-
IV. Rom. & Jul., Rich. II	-	3	1	47	26	30	11	4	-	122	53.1	68.9	-	2.5	0.8	38.5	21.3	24.6	9.0	3.3	-
V. King John, 1-2 Henry IV, Henry V, Jul. Caesar	1	3	8	99	74	73	40	6	1	305	48.1	59.3	0.3	1.0	2.6	32.5	24.5	23.9	13.1	2.0	0.3
VI. M. of Venice, Merry Wives, Much Ado	-	1	1	36	30	35	15	-	1	119	42.7	60.5	-	0.8	0.8	30.3	25.2	29.4	12.6	-	0.8

80

VII, As You Like It,	-	5	2	85	37	72	19	4	3	227	48.4	73.1	-	2.2	0.9	37.4	16.3	31.7	8.4	1.7	1.3
Tw. Night, Tr. & Cress.	3	8	6	155	51	159	51	10	6	449	43.2	73.9	0.7	1.8	1.3	34.5	11.4	35.4	11.4	2.2	1.3
VIII, Hamlet, Othello	-	-	5	64	16	136	44	30	3	298	24.5	77.2	-	-	1.7	21.4	5.4	45.6	14.6	10.1	1.0
IX, Measure for Meas., All's Well	-	9	5	123	58	282	104	18	5	604	25.1	71.5	-	1.5	0.8	20.4	9.6	46.7	17.2	3.0	0.8
X, Timon, Lear, Macbeth	1	4	6	116	94	362	190	39	33	845	16.9	61.7	0.1	0.4	0.7	13.8	11.1	42.8	22.5	4.6	3.9
XI, Ant. & Cleop., Coriolanus	-	6	5	165	134	421	206	54	20	1011	20.1	63.9	-	0.6	0.5	16.3	13.3	41.6	20.4	5.3	2.0
XII, Pericles (S.), Cymb., Winter's T., Tempest	1	-	2	37	35	113	80	14	16	298	15.2	55.0	0.3	-	0.7	12.4	11.7	37.9	26.8	4.7	5.4
XIII, Henry VIII (S.), Two Noble Kinsmen (S.)	-	2	5	28	68	49	40	7	-	199	26.7	44.7	-	2.5	1.0	14.1	34.2	24.6	20.1	3.5	-
Chapman, All Fools	4	15	9	100	97	101	82	9	-	417	40.0	54.0	0.9	3.6	2.2	24.0	23.3	24.2	19.6	2.2	-
Gentleman Usher	3	-	-	35	42	78	21	9	1	180	27.5	65.0	-	1.7	-	19.4	23.3	43.3	11.7	0.6	-
Monsieur d'Olive	-	1	-	10	9	15	14	3	-	52	25.6	55.8	-	1.9	-	19.4	17.3	28.7	26.9	5.8	-
Bussy d'Ambois	6	-	6	24	40	41	27	5	5	150	33.6	50.7	0.7	4.0	0.6	16.0	26.7	27.3	18.0	3.3	-
Charles Duke of Byron	1	1	4	28	39	51	39	5	5	167	25.8	52.8	-	2.4	-	16.8	23.3	30.5	23.3	3.0	-
Revenge of Bussy d'Ambois	-	2	5	28	39	51	39	5	-	199	26.7	44.7	-	2.5	1.0	14.1	34.2	24.6	20.1	3.5	-
Chabot, Admiral of France	9	3	-	28	32	66	43	20	2	203	23.5	60.6	-	4.4	1.5	13.8	15.8	32.5	21.2	9.8	1.0
Caesar's Pompey	2	1	-	15	49	29	30	9	-	135	20.9	40.7	-	1.5	0.7	11.1	36.3	21.5	22.2	6.7	-
Marston, 1, 2 Antonio and Mellida	6	5	-	21	16	2	8	7	7	75	50.0	68.0	1.3	8.0	6.7	28.0	8.9	21.3	2.7	10.7	9.3
Malcontent	5	3	1	12	7	7	4	2	2	45	51.2	62.2	2.2	11.1	6.7	26.7	8.9	15.6	15.6	8.9	4.4
Sophonisba	13	7	1	39	39	21	15	4	-	164	43.6	64.6	1.2	7.9	4.3	23.8	14.6	23.8	12.8	9.1	2.4
What You Will	1	1	-	8	7	5	-	1	-	23	56.3	60.9	-	4.3	-	34.8	21.8	21.8	4.3	8.7	4.3
Insatiate Countess	-	1	2	7	5	3	2	1	2	23	48.9	60.9	-	-	4.3	30.4	21.8	21.8	13.0	-	-
Jonson, Tale of the Tub	1	3	5	57	48	81	38	33	4	270	29.7	64.4	0.4	1.1	1.9	21.1	17.8	30.0	14.1	12.2	1.5
Case Is Altered	-	5	1	23	18	32	26	3	1	109	31.9	57.8	-	4.6	0.9	21.1	16.5	29.4	23.9	2.8	0.9
Every Man In His Humour (1601)	-	1	2	6	2	2	3	2	1	19	50.0	55.0	-	-	-	31.6	10.5	10.5	15.8	2.8	5.3
Every Man In His Humour (1616)	1	2	-	15	6	11	2	1	3	41	51.4	70.7	2.4	5.3	10.5	36.6	14.6	26.9	4.9	2.4	7.3
Every Man Out of His Humour (1600)	-	-	-	10	4	8	7	2	-	31	37.0	64.5	-	-	-	32.3	12.9	25.8	22.6	6.4	-
Every Man Out of His Humour (1616)	-	1	-	11	3	9	8	3	1	36	36.4	66.7	-	2.8	-	30.6	8.3	25.0	22.2	8.3	2.8

81

82

C — FIGURES (Continued)

| Title | Basic Figures | | | | | | | | | | Percentages | | | | | | | | | | |
	1	2	3	4	5	6	7	8	9	Total	First Half	Even	1	2	3	4	5	6	7	8	9
Poetaster	-	3	-	13	10	12	4	2	1	45	45.7	66.7	-	6.7	-	28.9	22.2	26.7	8.9	4.4	2.2
Sejanus	6	14	10	83	89	128	85	39	44	498	27.6	53.0	1.2	2.8	2.0	16.7	17.9	25.7	17.1	7.8	8.8
Volpone	4	25	23	119	149	153	123	109	63	768	27.6	52.9	0.5	3.3	3.0	15.5	19.4	19.9	16.0	14.2	8.2
Alchemist	6	29	29	174	182	163	163	109	78	933	31.7	50.9	0.6	3.1	3.1	18.6	19.5	17.5	17.5	11.7	8.4
Catiline	3	20	9	81	88	121	92	47	33	494	27.8	54.6	0.6	4.0	1.8	16.4	17.8	24.5	18.6	9.5	6.7
Devil Is an Ass	4	28	33	118	120	147	104	72	43	669	33.3	54.6	0.6	4.2	4.9	17.6	17.9	22.0	15.5	10.8	6.4
Staple of News	2	25	12	107	127	131	131	75	30	640	28.5	54.1	0.3	3.9	1.9	16.7	19.8	20.5	20.5	11.6	4.7
New Inn	4	22	18	90	107	124	79	45	21	510	33.3	55.1	0.8	4.3	3.5	17.6	21.0	24.3	15.5	8.8	4.1
Magnetic Lady	2	14	9	68	73	110	81	29	16	402	28.6	55.0	0.5	3.5	2.2	16.9	18.2	27.4	20.1	7.2	4.0
Sad Shepherd	-	3	3	27	33	26	19	11	4	126	35.5	53.2	-	2.4	2.4	21.4	26.2	20.6	15.1	8.7	3.2
Heywood, Four Prentices of London	1	6	5	38	20	21	23	3	5	122	49.0	55.7	0.8	5.1	4.1	31.1	16.4	17.1	18.9	2.5	4.9
1 Edward IV	-	2	1	14	10	6	2	1	-	36	65.4	63.9	-	5.5	2.8	38.9	27.8	16.7	5.5	2.8	-
2 Edward IV	-	-	-	36	12	8	6	3	-	65	67.9	72.3	-	-	-	55.4	18.5	12.3	9.2	4.6	-
Royal King and Loyal Subject	-	3	4	45	20	66	33	-	-	171	34.4	66.7	-	1.8	2.3	26.3	11.7	38.6	19.3	-	-
Woman Killed with Kindness	-	2	-	37	14	27	13	5	1	99	45.9	71.7	-	2.0	-	37.4	14.1	27.3	13.1	5.1	1.0
Wise Woman of Hogsdon	-	3	1	10	5	30	20	2	-	71	21.2	63.4	-	4.2	1.4	14.1	7.0	42.3	28.2	2.8	-
If You Know Not Me	-	1	2	28	17	32	9	2	-	91	41.9	69.2	-	1.1	2.2	30.7	18.7	35.2	9.9	2.1	-
Rape of Lucrece	1	7	9	25	17	33	33	4	2	131	36.8	52.7	0.8	5.3	6.9	19.1	13.0	25.2	25.2	3.1	1.5
Golden Age	1	5	3	30	23	39	43	1	-	145	32.0	51.7	0.7	3.4	2.1	20.7	15.9	26.9	29.7	0.7	-
Silver Age	1	3	2	27	27	39	26	2	-	127	33.0	55.9	0.8	2.4	1.6	21.3	21.3	30.7	20.4	1.6	-
Brazen Age	-	6	4	46	31	31	27	1	2	148	47.9	56.8	-	4.1	2.7	31.1	20.9	20.9	18.2	0.7	1.4
1 Iron Age	2	5	2	32	20	56	34	6	1	158	29.7	62.7	1.3	3.2	1.3	20.2	12.7	35.4	21.5	3.8	0.6
2 Iron Age	-	2	4	13	35	81	106	5	3	249	8.8	40.6	-	0.8	1.6	5.2	14.1	32.5	42.6	2.0	1.2
Captives	-	3	3	25	23	125	219	9	10	417	7.9	38.8	-	0.7	0.7	6.0	5.5	30.0	52.5	2.2	2.4
1, 2 Fair Maid of the West	1	7	9	68	42	152	177	9	4	469	20.0	50.3	0.2	1.5	1.9	14.5	9.0	32.4	37.7	1.9	0.9
English Traveller	1	3	7	32	22	122	231	15	1	434	10.4	39.6	0.2	0.7	1.6	7.4	5.1	28.1	53.2	3.5	0.2
Maidenhead Well Lost	-	12	4	54	26	76	54	7	4	237	33.2	62.9	-	5.1	1.7	22.8	11.0	32.0	22.8	3.0	1.7
Challenge for Beauty	2	9	6	32	16	62	118	10	6	261	20.0	43.3	0.8	3.4	2.3	12.3	6.1	23.8	45.2	3.8	2.3
Pleasant Dialogues and Dramas (blank verse plays)	-	3	2	13	9	52	81	2	-	162	11.7	43.2	-	1.9	1.2	8.0	5.5	32.2	50.0	1.2	-

Dekker, Shoemakers' Holiday	-	4	1	23	19	39	9	3	-	98	35.4	70.4	-	4.1	1.0	23.5	19.4	39.8	9.2	3.0	-
Old Fortunatus	-	-	1	10	15	19	4	1	-	50	31.4	60.0	-	-	2.0	20.0	30.0	38.0	8.0	2.0	-
Patient Grissel (D. acc. to Hunt) (no split lines in remainder)	-	5	1	16	16	34	14	1	1	88	30.6	63.6	-	5.7	1.1	18.2	18.2	38.6	15.9	1.1	1.1
Satiromastix	1	3	1	15	7	15	7	13	2	64	35.1	71.9	1.6	4.7	1.6	23.4	10.9	23.4	10.9	20.3	3.1
Sir Thomas Wyatt (D. acc. to Greg)	-	1	-	8	7	10	2	-	-	28	42.9	67.9	-	3.6	-	28.6	25.0	35.7	7.1	-	-
(Webster acc. to Greg)	-	2	1	9	-	17	1	2	-	32	38.7	93.7	-	6.2	3.1	28.1	-	53.2	3.1	6.2	-
1 Honest Whore (D. acc. to Bullen)	-	8	5	24	15	38	19	7	2	118	35.9	65.3	-	6.8	4.2	20.3	12.7	32.2	16.1	5.9	1.7
(Middleton acc. to Bullen)	-	1	-	3	6	13	5	-	-	28	18.2	57.1	-	3.6	-	10.7	21.4	46.4	17.9	-	-
2 Honest Whore	1	4	3	31	15	51	27	9	-	141	30.7	67.3	0.7	2.8	2.1	22.0	10.6	36.2	19.1	6.4	-
Whore of Babylon	2	14	14	47	41	88	57	36	14	313	28.3	59.1	0.6	4.5	4.5	15.0	13.1	28.1	18.2	11.5	4.5
Roaring Girl (D. acc. to Bullen)	4	6	2	16	14	36	20	3	1	102	31.8	59.8	3.9	5.9	2.0	15.7	13.7	35.3	19.6	2.9	1.0
(Middleton acc. to Bullen)	1	5	3	17	20	60	30	10	10	156	19.1	59.0	0.6	3.2	1.9	10.9	12.8	38.5	19.2	6.4	6.4
If This Be Not a Good Play	5	21	12	83	45	89	48	27	10	340	41.0	64.7	1.5	6.2	3.5	24.4	13.2	26.2	14.1	7.9	2.9
Match Me in London	12	25	24	64	50	99	69	38	17	398	33.0	56.8	3.0	6.3	6.0	16.1	12.6	24.9	17.3	9.5	4.3
Virgin Martyr (D. acc. to Fleay)	1	1	1	6	6	14	6	7	1	43	27.0	65.1	2.3	2.3	2.3	14.0	14.0	32.6	14.0	16.3	2.3
(Massinger acc. to Fleay)	3	5	4	40	64	86	98	25	3	328	19.7	47.6	0.9	1.5	1.2	12.2	19.5	26.2	29.9	7.6	0.9
Witch of Edmonton (D. acc. to Hunt)	-	7	3	31	31	51	30	16	9	178	27.9	59.0	-	3.9	1.7	17.4	17.4	28.7	16.9	9.0	5.0
(Not D. acc. to Hunt)	-	3	2	13	13	14	17	6	4	72	13.7	50.0	-	4.2	2.8	18.1	18.1	19.4	23.6	8.3	5.6
Wonder of a Kingdom	2	8	7	43	27	66	51	14	2	220	31.1	59.1	0.9	3.6	3.2	19.5	12.3	30.0	23.2	6.4	0.9
Sun's Darling (D. acc. to Pierce)	1	5	4	12	11	28	24	6	6	97	25.6	52.6	1.0	5.2	4.1	12.4	11.3	28.9	24.7	6.2	6.2
(Ford acc. to Pierce and others)	1	4	2	9	8	20	12	3	6	65	28.1	54.4	1.5	6.2	3.1	13.8	12.3	30.8	18.5	4.6	9.2
Day, Law Tricks	1	20	11	71	76	48	20	16	-	263	55.1	58.9	0.4	7.6	4.2	27.0	28.9	18.2	7.6	6.1	-
Isle of Gulls	-	4	1	27	16	9	5	2	-	64	66.7	65.6	-	6.2	1.6	42.2	25.0	14.1	7.8	3.1	-
Humour Out of Breath	1	1	2	13	10	10	6	3	2	48	44.7	56.25	2.1	2.1	4.2	27.1	20.8	20.8	12.5	6.2	4.2
Parliament of Bees	1	8	4	20	20	29	14	8	3	107	37.9	60.7	0.9	7.5	3.7	18.7	18.7	27.1	13.1	7.5	2.8

C — FIGURES (Continued)

TITLE		BASIC FIGURES										First Half	Even	PERCENTAGES								
	1	2	3	4	5	6	7	8	9	Total			1	2	3	4	5	6	7	8	9
Fletcher,																					
Faithful Shepherdess	-	5	-	26	21	29	21	3	3	108	35.6	58.3	-	4.6	-	24.1	19.4	26.9	19.4	2.8	2.8
Cupid's Revenge	1	6	1	29	9	26	14	10	3	99	41.1	71.7	1.0	6.1	1.0	29.3	9.1	26.3	14.1	10.1	3.0
Philaster	-	1	1	16	7	14	7	2	-	48	43.9	68.7	-	2.1	2.1	33.3	14.6	29.2	14.6	4.2	-
Maid's Tragedy	1	3	1	8	10	17	14	8	2	64	24.1	56.2	1.6	4.7	1.6	12.5	15.6	26.6	21.9	12.5	3.1
King and No King	-	2	1	16	12	17	10	8	4	70	32.8	61.4	-	2.9	1.4	22.9	17.1	24.3	14.3	11.4	5.7
Woman's Prize	3	9	10	79	68	163	217	95	26	670	16.8	51.6	0.4	1.3	1.5	11.8	10.1	24.3	32.3	14.2	3.9
Captain	-	6	9	52	83	94	95	37	15	391	21.8	48.3	-	1.5	2.3	13.3	21.2	24.0	24.3	9.5	3.9
Scornful Lady (Chambers)	-	1	-	28	14	15	15	8	4	85	40.8	61.2	-	1.2	-	32.9	16.5	17.6	17.6	9.4	4.7
Henry VIII (Chambers)	-	4	1	26	28	51	69	37	4	220	16.1	53.7	-	1.8	0.5	11.8	12.7	23.2	31.4	16.8	1.8
Two Noble Kinsmen (Chambers)																					
Bonduca	4	4	12	39	55	78	82	34	15	323	22.0	48.0	1.2	1.2	3.7	12.1	17.0	24.1	25.4	10.5	4.6
Valentinian	2	7	8	83	59	135	182	76	37	589	18.9	51.1	0.3	1.2	1.4	14.1	10.0	22.9	30.9	12.9	6.3
Wit Without Money	2	6	3	64	42	123	180	106	24	550	14.8	54.6	0.4	1.1	0.5	11.6	7.6	22.4	32.6	19.3	4.4
Monsieur Thomas	1	3	13	85	49	149	128	56	13	497	22.8	59.0	0.2	0.6	2.6	17.1	9.9	30.0	25.7	11.3	2.6
Mad Lover	1	8	13	100	71	167	125	107	15	607	22.8	62.9	0.2	1.3	2.1	16.4	11.7	27.5	20.6	17.6	2.5
Loyal Subject	4	5	12	96	86	154	174	115	43	689	19.4	53.7	0.6	0.7	1.7	13.9	12.5	22.3	25.3	16.7	6.2
Humorous Lieutenant	-	5	3	93	52	185	121	73	9	541	20.7	65.8	-	0.9	0.6	17.2	9.6	34.2	22.4	13.5	1.7
Women Pleased	1	7	5	139	51	233	132	102	16	686	23.9	70.1	0.1	1.0	0.7	20.3	7.4	34.0	19.2	14.9	2.3
Wild-Goose Chase	2	8	6	107	46	138	73	52	5	437	31.5	69.8	0.5	1.8	1.4	24.5	10.5	31.6	16.7	11.9	1.1
Island Princess	1	-	5	108	43	175	114	64	11	521	24.3	67.2	0.2	-	1.0	20.7	8.3	33.6	21.9	12.3	2.1
Pilgrim	-	4	3	60	30	176	69	61	7	410	17.4	72.4	-	1.0	0.7	14.6	7.3	42.9	16.8	14.9	2.0
Have a Wife	1	4	4	124	44	180	83	50	6	496	29.2	72.2	0.2	0.8	0.6	25.0	8.9	36.3	16.7	10.1	1.4
Wife for a Month	-	6	-	111	47	125	29	33	4	355	38.0	77.5	-	1.7	-	31.3	13.2	35.2	8.2	9.3	1.1
Fletcher with Massinger,																					
Little French Lawyer (F)	-	6	1	75	36	125	66	46	7	362	25.2	69.6	-	1.6	0.3	20.7	9.9	34.5	18.2	12.7	1.9
(M)	-	-	3	50	48	78	72	32	3	286	22.3	55.9	-	-	1.0	17.5	16.8	27.3	25.2	11.2	1.0
Barnavelt (F)	-	1	2	61	20	70	38	35	5	232	30.2	71.1	-	0.4	0.8	26.3	8.6	30.2	16.4	15.1	2.2
(M)	-	-	1	24	34	22	36	10	3	130	26.0	43.1	-	-	0.8	18.5	26.2	16.9	27.7	7.7	2.3
False One (F)	-	2	2	41	30	65	45	28	5	218	23.8	62.4	-	0.9	0.9	18.8	13.8	29.8	20.6	12.8	2.3
(M)	-	1	3	24	16	47	51	12	2	156	20.0	53.8	-	0.6	1.9	15.4	10.3	30.1	32.7	7.7	1.3
Double Marriage (F)	1	4	3	93	24	132	62	55	9	383	28.1	74.2	0.3	1.0	0.8	24.3	6.3	34.5	16.2	14.3	2.3
(M)	1	3	4	32	40	64	70	14	1	229	21.2	49.3	0.4	1.3	1.7	14.0	17.5	27.9	30.6	6.1	0.4

Play	1	2	3	4	5	6	7	8	9	10	11	12	13	14	15	16	17	18	19	20	21
Custom of Country (F)	-	5	1	67	28	104	36	40	4	285	28.4	75.8	-	1.8	0.4	23.5	9.8	36.5	12.6	14.0	1.4
(M)	1	1	3	17	40	44	59	18	3	186	15.1	43.0	0.5	0.5	1.6	9.1	21.5	23.7	31.7	9.7	1.6
Sea-Voyage (F)	1	10	2	52	20	58	29	31	7	210	34.2	71.9	0.5	4.8	1.0	24.8	9.5	27.6	13.8	14.8	3.3
(M)	-	3	4	23	19	36	21	9	3	118	30.3	52.5	-	2.5	3.4	18.7	16.1	30.5	17.8	7.6	2.5
Prophetess (F)	-	2	-	47	25	80	51	37	9	251	21.7	66.1	-	0.8	-	18.7	10.0	31.9	20.3	14.7	3.6
(M)	-	1	-	14	29	46	30	10	3	133	14.4	53.4	-	0.8	0.3	10.2	21.8	34.6	22.5	7.5	2.3
Spanish Curate (F)	1	2	1	58	33	104	59	37	8	302	22.7	66.2	0.3	0.3	0.4	19.3	10.9	34.4	19.5	12.3	2.6
(M)	-	1	1	31	39	90	65	12	4	244	16.6	55.3	-	0.8	0.4	12.7	16.0	36.9	26.6	4.9	1.6
Massinger, Duke of Milan	1	2	3	64	92	139	149	36	2	488	17.7	49.9	0.2	0.4	0.6	13.1	18.9	28.5	30.5	7.4	0.4
Bondman	-	2	7	62	94	135	182	46	4	531	16.0	46.0	-	0.2	1.3	11.7	17.7	25.4	34.3	8.7	0.8
Renegado	1	4	7	36	94	100	164	45	6	457	13.2	40.5	0.2	0.9	1.5	7.9	20.6	21.9	35.9	9.8	1.3
Maid of Honour	-	3	5	49	105	122	185	54	6	529	13.4	43.1	-	0.6	0.9	9.3	19.8	23.1	35.0	10.2	1.1
Parliament of Love	-	1	2	41	70	75	127	27	-	343	16.1	42.0	-	0.3	0.5	11.9	20.4	21.9	37.0	7.9	-
New Way to Pay Old Debts	-	10	6	77	142	111	131	35	6	518	25.0	45.0	-	1.9	1.2	14.9	27.4	21.4	25.3	6.8	1.2
Roman Actor	-	5	5	37	92	94	122	19	9	379	15.0	39.8	-	0.3	1.3	9.8	24.3	24.8	32.2	5.0	2.4
Unnatural Combat	1	5	7	42	93	88	139	27	8	409	17.1	39.6	-	1.2	1.7	10.3	22.7	25.1	34.0	6.6	2.0
Great Duke of Florence	1	7	7	64	91	125	171	34	5	498	17.7	44.8	0.2	-	1.4	12.9	18.3	25.1	34.3	6.8	1.0
Picture	-	5	5	70	121	116	191	35	8	550	18.4	40.9	-	0.7	0.9	12.7	22.0	20.9	34.8	6.4	1.5
Emperor of the East	-	4	2	47	78	112	197	32	5	476	13.3	41.0	-	0.8	0.4	9.9	16.4	25.1	41.4	6.7	0.8
Believe as You List	-	4	5	47	87	122	167	50	5	487	14.0	45.8	-	0.8	1.0	9.6	17.9	25.1	34.3	10.3	1.0
City Madam	-	12	12	85	113	156	205	37	3	623	20.2	45.6	-	1.0	1.9	13.6	18.1	25.0	32.9	5.9	1.4
Guardian	-	5	9	78	115	122	178	51	4	564	20.9	45.4	0.4	0.9	1.6	13.8	20.4	21.6	31.6	9.0	0.9
Bashful Lover	1	5	5	68	75	106	144	54	7	462	19.6	49.8	0.2	0.4	1.1	14.7	16.2	22.9	31.2	11.7	1.5
Beaumont, Woman Hater (Chambers)	-	2	1	14	6	18	11	7	2	61	30.9	67.2	-	3.3	1.6	23.0	9.8	29.5	18.0	11.5	3.3
Knight of the Burning Pestle	-	1	7	15	23	17	8	-	-	71	14.5	54.9	-	1.4	-	9.9	21.1	32.4	23.9	11.3	-
Cupid's Revenge	-	3	8	13	18	17	12	4	2	77	40.7	48.1	-	3.9	10.4	16.9	23.4	22.1	15.6	5.2	2.6
Philaster	-	13	8	47	40	43	22	14	1	189	46.3	62.9	0.5	6.9	4.2	24.9	21.2	22.7	11.6	7.4	0.5
Maid's Tragedy	-	10	13	79	60	100	52	17	3	335	37.5	61.5	0.3	3.0	3.9	23.6	17.9	29.9	15.5	5.0	0.9
King and no King	-	15	13	56	53	73	36	28	8	283	31.9	60.8	0.4	5.3	4.6	19.8	18.7	25.8	12.7	9.9	2.8
Scornful Lady (Chambers)																					
Middleton, Family of Love (Chambers)	-	6	8	23	7	22	12	10	2	90	28.6	67.8	-	6.7	8.9	25.6	7.8	24.4	13.3	11.1	2.2
Phoenix	-	1	-	8	2	5	3	1	1	20	50.0	75.0	-	5.0	-	40.0	10.0	25.0	15.0	5.0	-
Michaelmas Term	-	5	3	23	13	34	22	7	2	110	33.0	62.7	0.9	4.5	2.7	20.9	11.8	30.9	20.0	6.4	1.8
Mad World, My Masters	-	3	2	9	16	15	2	2	-	49	22.5	49.0	-	2.0	4.1	12.2	18.4	30.6	28.6	4.1	-
Your Five Gallants	-	2	4	28	16	34	11	8	1	106	40.0	68.9	1.0	2.8	3.8	26.4	15.1	32.0	10.4	7.5	1.0
Trick to Catch the Old One	-	2	5	12	15	13	6	2	-	55	30.4	52.7	-	-	3.6	21.8	16.4	27.3	23.6	3.6	3.6

C — FIGURES (Continued)

Title	Basic Figures												Percentages								
	1	2	3	4	5	6	7	8	9	Total	First Half	Even	1	2	3	4	5	6	7	8	9
Chaste Maid in Cheapside	-	8	7	52	42	161	103	20	2	395	19.0	61.0	-	2.0	1.8	13.2	10.6	40.8	26.1	5.1	0.5
Witch	4	3	4	27	36	100	72	7	2	254	17.4	54.0	1.6	1.2	1.6	10.6	14.2	39.4	28.3	2.8	0.4
No Wit, No Help	1	7	7	44	44	90	85	11	7	296	23.4	52.1	0.3	2.4	2.4	14.8	14.8	30.4	28.7	3.7	2.3
More Dissemblers	-	1	7	29	32	71	59	8	2	209	20.9	52.2	-	0.5	3.3	13.9	15.3	34.0	28.2	3.8	1.0
Widow	4	10	7	50	56	128	101	10	3	369	22.7	53.7	1.1	2.7	1.9	13.6	15.2	34.7	27.4	2.7	0.8
Hengist	2	15	7	47	34	90	89	19	3	306	26.5	55.9	0.7	4.9	2.6	15.4	11.1	29.4	29.1	6.2	0.7
Women Beware Women	3	8	10	46	47	123	93	14	1	345	22.5	55.4	0.9	2.3	2.9	13.3	13.6	35.6	27.0	4.1	0.3
Changeling (Rowley) (M)	-	2	1	19	14	28	16	6	2	88	29.7	62.5	-	2.3	1.1	21.6	15.9	31.8	18.2	6.8	2.3
Game at Chess	2	3	8	21	28	62	73	-	3	200	19.8	44.0	1.0	1.5	4.0	10.5	14.0	31.0	36.5	-	1.5
Middleton (?), Second Maiden's Tragedy	4	3	3	28	32	72	88	7	1	238	18.4	46.2	1.7	1.3	1.3	11.8	13.4	30.3	37.0	2.9	0.4
Webster, White Devil	1	5	8	62	83	117	110	28	11	425	22.2	49.9	0.2	1.2	1.9	14.6	19.5	27.5	25.9	6.6	2.6
Duchess of Malfi	2	16	22	78	85	104	93	30	14	444	32.9	51.4	0.5	3.6	5.0	17.6	19.1	23.4	20.9	6.8	3.2
Devil's Law Case	1	7	20	65	53	91	79	18	11	345	31.8	52.5	0.3	2.0	5.8	18.8	15.4	26.4	22.9	5.2	3.2
Anything for Quiet Life (W) (Middleton) *(Only four line splits)*	-	3	2	10	18	18	26	4	1	82	23.4	42.7	-	3.7	2.4	12.2	21.9	21.9	31.7	4.9	1.2
Fair Maid of Inn (W)	-	2	7	15	26	24	34	7	2	117	26.4	41.0	-	1.7	6.0	12.8	22.2	20.5	29.1	6.0	1.7
(Massinger)	-	6	1	17	31	22	43	9	5	134	23.3	40.3	-	4.5	0.7	12.7	23.1	16.4	32.1	6.7	3.7
(Ford)	-	4	4	11	13	21	40	13	4	110	19.6	44.5	-	3.6	3.6	10.0	11.8	19.1	36.4	11.8	3.6
Cure for a Cuckold (W)	2	-	-	11	18	28	35	11	3	108	14.4	46.3	1.8	-	-	10.2	16.7	25.9	32.4	10.2	2.8
(Heywood)	-	1	1	1	4	7	12	1	-	27	13.0	37.0	-	3.7	3.7	3.7	14.8	25.9	44.4	3.7	-
Appius and Virginia (W)	-	2	2	16	23	33	38	5	2	121	16.5	46.3	-	1.7	1.7	13.2	19.0	27.3	31.4	4.1	1.7
(Heywood)	1	3	4	17	15	21	31	4	1	97	30.5	46.4	1.0	3.1	4.1	17.5	15.5	21.6	32.0	4.1	1.0
Tourneur or Middleton (?), Revenger's Tragedy	1	8	6	58	27	59	63	16	5	243	33.8	58.0	0.4	3.3	2.5	23.9	11.1	24.3	25.9	6.6	2.1
Tourneur, Atheist's Tragedy	-	7	9	24	25	23	18	11	11	128	38.8	50.8	-	5.5	7.0	18.7	19.5	18.0	14.1	8.6	8.6
Ford, Lover's Melancholy	1	6	8	46	48	104	93	39	6	351	21.3	55.5	0.3	1.7	2.3	13.1	13.7	29.6	26.5	11.1	1.7
'Tis Pity She's a Whore	2	8	7	54	39	75	47	10	2	244	34.6	60.2	0.8	3.3	2.9	22.1	16.0	30.7	19.3	4.1	0.8
Broken Heart	3	11	12	55	63	142	147	51	22	506	18.3	51.2	0.6	2.2	2.4	10.8	12.5	28.1	29.0	10.1	4.3
Love's Sacrifice	1	10	4	35	37	52	50	26	6	221	27.2	55.7	0.5	4.5	1.8	15.9	16.7	23.5	22.6	11.8	2.7

Title	-	8	7	26	37	89	113	52	9	341	13.5	51.3	-	2.3	2.1	7.6	10.9	26.1	33.1	15.2	2.6
Perkin Warbeck	1	11	6	33	60	104	139	46	24	424	14.0	45.8	0.2	2.6	1.4	7.8	14.2	24.6	32.8	10.8	5.6
Fancies Chaste and Noble	2	3	5	63	50	122	125	52	20	442	18.6	54.3	0.5	0.7	1.1	14.2	11.3	27.6	28.3	11.8	4.5
Lady's Trial	2	9	4	84	41	90	67	34	6	337	33.4	64.4	0.6	2.7	1.2	24.9	12.2	26.7	19.9	10.1	1.8
Brome, New Academy	'	5	1	31	28	37	25	9	2	138	33.6	59.4	-	3.6	0.7	22.5	20.3	26.8	18.1	6.5	1.5
Court Beggar	1	1	1	46	38	62	32	6	1	188	32.7	61.2	0.5	0.5	0.5	24.5	20.2	33.0	17.0	3.2	0.5
Novella	'	10	3	54	28	63	26	12	3	199	39.2	69.3	-	5.0	1.5	27.1	14.1	31.7	13.1	6.0	1.5
Queen and Concubine	'	10	4	52	35	87	65	6	6	260	29.3	59.6	-	3.8	1.5	20.0	13.5	33.5	25.0	2.3	0.4
English Moor	2	6	7	76	50	95	58	23	1	323	33.3	61.9	0.6	1.9	2.2	23.5	15.5	29.4	18.0	7.1	1.9
Love-Sick Court	1	5	1	41	27	63	47	14	19	200	27.7	61.5	0.5	2.5	0.5	20.5	13.5	31.5	23.5	7.0	0.5
Damoiselle	4	16	26	78	47	76	80	48	9	394	33.8	55.3	1.0	4.1	6.6	19.8	11.9	19.3	20.3	12.2	4.8
Shirley, Traitor	1	15	13	67	42	81	54	33	10	315	35.2	63.2	0.3	4.8	4.1	21.3	13.3	25.7	17.1	10.5	2.9
Hyde Park	'	21	23	87	71	94	118	75	14	499	30.6	55.5	-	4.2	4.6	17.4	14.2	18.9	23.6	15.0	2.0
Lady of Pleasure	'	10	10	47	29	65	67	50	2	290	25.7	58.6	-	3.4	3.4	16.2	10.0	21.7	23.1	17.3	4.8
Cardinal	'	4	1	19	1	13	2	3	1	45	54.5	86.7	-	8.9	2.2	42.2	28.9	28.3	4.4	6.7	4.4
Davenant, Cruel Brother	'	5	4	10	4	13	3	6	3	46	45.2	73.9	-	10.9	8.7	21.7	8.7	28.3	6.5	13.0	2.2
Albovine	'	18	2	51	5	63	4	20	5	166	44.1	91.6	-	10.8	1.2	30.7	3.0	38.0	2.4	12.0	1.8
Just Italian	'	5	5	51	12	58	7	6	-	144	46.2	83.3	-	3.5	3.5	35.4	8.3	40.3	4.8	4.2	'
Wits	'	6	6	77	36	85	61	21	5	297	34.1	63.6	-	2.0	3.5	25.9	12.1	28.6	20.5	7.1	1.7
News from Plymouth	'	6	'	30	4	44	2	6	'	92	40.9	93.5	-	6.5	1.3	32.6	4.3	47.8	2.2	6.5	'
Platonic Lover	'	3	1	33	4	31	'	4	'	76	51.4	93.4	-	3.9	1.8	43.4	5.3	40.8	'	5.3	'
Distresses	'	9	1	20	1	21	1	3	'	56	57.5	94.6	-	16.1	3.3	35.7	1.8	37.5	1.8	5.4	'
Fair Favourite	'	1	1	9	6	10	1	2	'	30	45.8	73.3	-	3.3		30.0	20.0	33.3	3.3	6.7	'
Playhouse to be Let	'																				
Siege	'	5	7	26	10	17	16	8	3	92	42.7	60.9	-	5.4	7.6	28.3	10.9	18.5	17.4	8.7	3.2

COMPARISON OF SHAKESPEAREAN RUN-ON LINES
WITH PAUSES IN SECOND HALF-LINES

Play	RUN-ON LINES (Koenig's figures)	PAUSES IN 2ND HALF-LINE IN RELATION TO PAUSES IN 1ST HALF-LINE		
		All Punctuation Marks	Strong Pauses	Line Splits
Titus Andronicus (TA)	12.0	30.8	34.2	33.3
Comedy of Errors (CE)	12.9	38.4	42.9	41.7
1 Henry VI (1 H VI)	10.4	32.4	27.1	53.3
2 Henry VI (2 H VI)	11.4	36.4	35.5	36.4
3 Henry VI (3 H VI)	9.5	32.7	33.5	41.7
Taming of the Shrew (TS)	8.1	31.7	34.1	41.0
Richard III (R III)	13.2	37.5	35.7	25.0
Two Gentlemen of Verona (TGV)	12.4	35.1	35.0	33.3
Love's Labour's Lost (LLL)	18.4	37.8	36.5	26.5
Midsummer-Night's Dream (MND)	13.2	39.4	42.1	46.2
Romeo & Juliet (RJ)	14.2	37.9	38.0	51.5
Richard II (R II)	19.9	39.8	42.2	36.7
King John (KJ)	17.7	41.3	41.2	40.0
Merchant of Venice (MV)	21.5	48.3	42.0	62.5
1 Henry IV (1 H IV)	28.8	46.5	47.0	53.1
2 Henry IV (2 H IV)	21.4	43.9	49.5	63.3
Merry Wives of Windsor (MW)	20.1	43.8	47.3	38.5
Much Ado About Nothing (MA)	19.3	46.0	56.1	59.3
Henry V (HV)	21.8	50.6	56.5	53.8
Julius Caesar (JC)	19.3	48.2	56.9	53.1
As You Like It (AYL)	17.1	47.5	52.3	65.5
Twelfth Night (TN)	14.7	53.8	57.4	42.3
Hamlet (Ham)	23.1	52.2	57.9	57.7
Troilus & Cressida (TC)	27.4	45.4	48.1	47.9
Measure for Measure (MM)	23.0	57.8	63.2	68.1
Othello (Oth)	19.5	50.8	49.1	56.1
All's Well that Ends Well (AW)	28.4	65.5	73.2	77.5
Timon of Athens (Tim)	32.5	60.9	68.7	71.5
King Lear (Lear)	29.3	64.7	67.0	73.2
Macbeth (Mac)	36.6	68.6	72.3	78.9
Pericles (Per)	25.0	68.6	72.2	75.0
Antony & Cleopatra (AC)	43.3	70.4	76.1	81.1
Coriolanus (Cor)	45.9	70.2	78.0	85.4
Cymbeline (Cym)	46.0	70.0	76.1	80.0
Winter's Tale (WT)	37.5	68.7	74.7	79.8
Tempest (Tem)	41.5	66.4	75.4	81.0
Henry VIII (H VIII)	39.0	74.8	79.6	85.2

A NOTE ON THE SOURCES

The texts used in this study—complete works unless otherwise indicated—were examined in the following editions.

FOR THE FOREIGN POETS: Saint-Hilaire's edition of Eustache Deschamps (1878), vol. I, pp. 69-99; E. Hoepffner's Guillaume de Machaut (1908), vol. I, "Le Jugement dou Roy de Behaingne," lines 1-1000; Pierre Jannet's Clément Marot (1868), vol. II, "Complaintes," pp. 240-260; Henri Chamand's Du Bellay (1910), vol. II, "Les Antiquitez de Rome," "Songe," "Les Amours"; Prosper Blanchemain's Ronsard (1857), vol. I, "Les Amours," Premier Livre I-XXX; Petrarca, *Rime*, ed. F. Neri (1951), Rime I-CC; Boccaccio, *La Teseide* (Biblioteca Scelta, 1837), cantos I-IV; Ariosto, *Orlando Furioso* (Firenze, 1882), cantos I-III; Tasso, *Opere* (Pisa, 1830), vol. XXVI, cantos I-II of *La Gerusalemme Liberata*.

FOR THE ENGLISH POETS: F. N. Robinson's Chaucer (1933); R. K. Root's *Troilus and Criseyde* (1932), books I-II; Henry Bergen's edition of Lydgate's *Troy Book* (E.E.T.S., 1906), I.1-1028; Robert Henryson's *Fables and Poems*, ed. H. Harvey Wood (1938), "The Testament of Cresseid"; Hoccleve's *Regiment of Princes*, ed. F. J. Furnivall (E.E.T.S., 1897), stanzas 1-75; A. Dyce's Skelton (1843), "The Bowge of Court"; Padelford's Surrey (1928), the First Book of the Aeneid according to MS Hargrave 205; *Songs and Sonnets* (Tottel's Miscellany), ed. Hyder Rollins (1928-29), for the poems of Wyatt, Surrey, and Grimald (the text of Tottel's Miscellany rather than that of the extant MS versions was chosen for Wyatt because that was the form in which Wyatt was known to Elizabethan readers and in which he influenced them); *The Mirror for Magistrates*, ed. Lily B. Campbell (1938) for Sackville's contributions; J. W. Cunliffe's Gascoigne (1907-10); A. Feuillerat's Sidney (1922-26); the Johns Hopkins Variorum Spenser; *Early English Classical Tragedies*, ed. J. W. Cunliffe (1912), for *Iocasta*, *Gismond of Salerne*, and *The Misfortunes of Arthur*; the Tudor Facsimile Texts editions of Gorboduc and Marlowe's *Dr. Faustus*; the Malone Society reprints of *Tancred and Gismund*, all of Peele's and Greene's plays, Lodge and Greene's *A Looking Glass for London*, Lodge's *Wounds of Civil War*, Marlowe's *Edward II*, *Arden of Feversham*, *Selimus*, *George a Greene*, *Caesar's Revenge*, *Sir John Oldcastle*, *A Larum for London*, *The Weakest Goeth to the Wall*, *A Trial of Chivalry*, Kyd's *Spanish Tragedy* (1952 ed.), Thomas Heywood's *If You Know Not Me* and *The Captives*, Marston's *Antonio and Mellida* (both parts), Jonson's *Every Man Out of his Humour* (1600 ed.), Middleton's *Witch*, John Day's *Law Tricks*, *The Second Maiden's Tragedy*, Massinger's *Believe as You List* and *The Parliament of Love*, Fletcher's *Bonduca*; the Bodley Head Quarto of Marston's *Scourge of Villanie* (1599 ed.); the Chatto and Windus facsimile edition of Shakespeare's First Folio (1876); H. Littledale's edition of *The Two Noble Kinsmen* (N.S.S., 1876-85); the Pearson editions of Chapman, Heywood, Brome, and Dekker (for *The Sun's Darling*); Fredson Bowers' Dekker (1953—); Herford and Simpson's Ben Jonson (1925-52); H. Harvey Wood's Marston (1934-39); G. Bullough's Greville (1939); A. H. Bullen's Middleton (1885-86); R. C. Bald's editions of Middleton's *A Game at Chess* (1929) and *Hengist* (1938); Sir Herbert Grierson's Donne (Oxford Standard Authors, 1949); Allardyce Nicoll's Tourneur (1930); F. L. Lucas's Webster (1927); Waller and Glover's Beaumont and Fletcher (1905-12); McKerrow's edition of Fletcher's *Wit Without Money* in the Variorum Beaumont and Fletcher (1905), vol. II; J. M. Mason's Massinger (1829); the edition of Massinger's *Roman Actor* by W. L. Sandidge, Jr. (1929), that of his *Unnatural Combat* by R. S. Telfer (1932), and of his *City Madam* by R. Kirk (1934); the Mermaid Ford, Shirley, and Massinger; Bullen's John Day (1881); William Paterson's edition of Davenant (1872). Photostats or microfilms of the earliest editions were used for the poems of Marlowe and Shakespeare: for Marlowe's *Tamburlaine* (both parts), *Dido, The Jew of Malta,* and *The Massacre at Paris;* for Lyly's *Woman in the Moon;* for *Pericles;* and for Chapman's *Pompey and Caesar* and *Chabot.*

My arrangement of Shakespeare's plays shows traces of the influence of Chambers, McManaway, and Karl Wentersdorf. My chronology of Beaumont and Webster is according to Eugene M. Waith, that of Middleton according to R. H. Barker. In the case of Dekker I follow Fredson Bowers, in that of Webster, F. L. Lucas. Elsewhere my main authorities on chronology are Chambers and T. M. Parrott.

In problems of authorship I generally follow Chambers, but many of Oliphant's views concerning the collaboration of Fletcher and Massinger have been taken into account. I have avoided plays with too tangled problems of collaboration. The distribution of authorship in the plays in which Webster collaborated is according to F. L. Lucas. The names placed in parentheses after titles preceding the statistical matter in my tabular section indicate additional reliance on students of authorship.

UNIVERSITY OF FLOR A MONOGRAP ..

Humanities

No. 1 (Sp) ıg 1959): *The Uncollected Let rs of
James Gat Percival*
Edited by arry R. Warfel

No. 2 (F₂ `59). *eigh H 's ography
The Earliest etche*
Edited by Step en F. ı le

No. 3 (Winter ı96 : *Pause Patterns in
Elizabethan and Jacobean rama*
By Ants Oras